SPOTLIGHT

SPOTLIGHT and INSIGHT

English for the Certificate:
Students' and Teacher's Book for each

IN THE PICTURE

Lower secondary material:
Core, Consolidation, Extension and Teacher's Book for each year

Details of all these books are available from the publishers.

SPOTLIGHT

Peter Chilver
Head of English Department, Langdon School, East Ham

Stanley Thornes (Publishers) Ltd

First published in 1987 by:
Stanley Thornes (Publishers) Ltd
Old Station Drive
Leckhampton
CHELTENHAM GL53 0DN
England

Reprinted 1987

British Library Cataloguing in Publication Data

Chilver, Peter
    Spotlight.—(Stanley Thornes English programme)
    Student's book
    1. English language—Grammar—1950-
    I. Title
    428   PE1112

ISBN 0-85950-567-7

Typeset by Tech-Set, Gateshead, Tyne & Wear.
Printed and bound in Great Britain by Butler and Tanner Ltd, Frome.

Contents

This list gives a **guide to texts** (including extracts) and other materials, and to **principal activities**.
All the Units offer opportunities for group and class discussion.

ACTIVITIES include answering questions on all the texts, using the texts as a basis for talks given by students, and collecting materials for talks on other topics. This Unit is designed for small groups of students to work on independently.

SPOTLIGHT: MAIN OBJECTIVES

1. To offer materials for good average groups or classes preparing for the GCSE examinations in English. The only major difference between this and the companion volume *Insight* is that the level of linguistic difficulty of the texts is strictly controlled. Even so:

   a) within every Unit there is some literature that is linguistically more complex, and

   b) in general, the level of linguistic difficulty is raised as the students progress from one Unit to the next.

2. To stimulate work across the whole range of language activities – talking, listening, reading and writing.

3. To include work in literature alongside language, but on the basis that teachers will also introduce their classes to a range of literary texts whether for the English or the English Literature examinations.

4. To meet the need for a range of activities as required for examinations that are either entirely or partly based on coursework.

TALKING AND LISTENING

5. Every Unit offers opportunities for class and group discussion. Some Units (4, 8, 12, 16 and 18) are designed for students to explore mostly on their own, in small groups, with the minimum of teacher intervention.

6. Opportunities are given, and also models, for students to engage in talk of quite different kinds, including debate, formal and structured discussion, solving problems together, and anecdotal chat.

7. Use is also made of various kinds of role play and improvisation.

8. A number of passages are included for listening comprehension. Generally, these are linguistically complex, and it is intended that the discussion of such texts, after students have listened to them, should extend the students' confidence and competence in reading texts that they find difficult. So, through listening and discussing, they develop as readers.

READING

9. There is a wide variety in the kinds of text offered. They extend from fiction, poetry and drama, to news reports, memoirs, philosophical and scientific writing, biography, autobiography, letters and speeches.

10. Extensive use is made of literature written by students.

11. Students are constantly invited to question the texts they are reading, so that they become involved in using texts generally to find out something for themselves, and to pursue the answers to their own questions.

12. The process of reading is a matter of moving backwards and forwards from the whole to the part, and students need constantly to be encouraged to do this. So almost all the Units give the students practice not only in exploring a single passage but also in relating different passages on a common theme to each other, finding their common threads.

13. The materials for reading are designed not only to stimulate good talking and listening, but also to offer the students a range of models of different kinds which they can explore in their own writing.

WRITING

14. The writer's sense of an audience is a major influence on his or her writing. Hence the Units offer constant opportunities for students to write for and with each other.

15. Note-making is also a central part of writing, and the Units give regular encouragement to build on plans, notes and outlines. In particular, there is a constant emphasis on the structuring of written work.

16. Some exercises are offered in punctuation, and these will be of use to some classes at some times. Obviously, everything depends on the teacher's perception of the needs of the class.

WRITTEN COURSEWORK

17. The various Units give opportunities for students to read and discuss a range of different kinds of writing and to explore this range in their own writing. These include:

creative, descriptive and imaginative writing – stories, poems, plays, descriptions (Units 1, 3, 5, 7, 9, 10, 11 and 13);

discursive and argumentative writing, in which the writer explores issues in a more or less impartial manner (Units 2, 6, 9, 10 and 14);

informative or explanatory writing, in which the writer gives information from various sources (Units 8, 12, 15, 16, 17 and 18);

personal writing, in which the writer evaluates or narrates personal experiences (Units 9, 10 and 14);

persuasive writing, in which the writer seeks to win the reader to a particular point of view (Units 6, 16 and 18).

Of course all these kinds of writing to some measure overlap.

Additionally, all the Units give opportunities for students to show in their writing a detailed understanding of the various texts. This includes:

the writing of answers to different kinds of comprehension questions, together with

sustained writing in various forms such as reports, letters and debating speeches (see especially Units 2, 4, 6, 8, 10, 12, 14, 16, 17 and 18).

GCSE ASSESSMENT OBJECTIVES

18. Candidates should be able to:
    1 understand and convey information;
    2 understand, order and present facts, ideas and opinions;
    3 evaluate information in reading material and in other media, and select what is relevant to specific purposes;
    4 articulate experience and express what is felt and what is imagined;
    5 recognise implicit meaning and attitudes.

USING DICTIONARIES AND LIBRARIES

19. Regular encouragement is given to students to use dictionaries and also libraries.

CONCEPTUAL DEVELOPMENT

20. At different times the focus is on different concepts. These include irony, dramatic irony, imagery and symbolism. It is not intended that these should be seen by students as either simple or rigid concepts. Students need to experiment with their use, to question them, and to begin to make them their own.

1 Introductory

Stories come in many different forms, including novels, plays, films, songs, poems ... Here are some examples.

drawn for a radio play, Ceremonies of War, *by Robin Jacques*

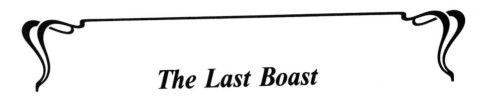

The Last Boast

When the time came for them to die, Pete Gossard cursed and Knife Hilton cried, but Wolfer Joe Kennedy yawned in the face of the hangman.

What he wanted to do was spit, to show he was not afraid, because he knew men would talk about him later and describe the end he made. But even Wolfer Joe could not raise enough saliva for spitting when he had a noose around his neck. The yawn was the next best thing.

Barney Gallagher, the United States deputy marshal, finished adjusting the rope and asked half-admiringly, 'Are we keeping you up?'

'Hanging me up, they told me,' Wolfer Joe answered.

On a packing box between his companions, he stood glaring out at the crowd of miners, with his lips pulled back from his teeth in the grin that was his trade-mark. He had foreseen the hour of his death, but not the way of it. He had felt the jar of the bullet, heard the Cheyenne arrow whir, gone down screaming under a grizzly's claws – all these were probabilities for a man who had lived as he had lived, and a man had to die sometime.

But he had always seen himself fighting to the end. He had not dreamed of an end by hanging, helpless, with his hands tied behind him. He would not give his executioners the satisfaction of knowing he was astonished. They were going to get satisfaction enough without that.

Knife Hilton stopped crying and stood drooping on his packing box, snuffling like a baby. Pete Gossard stopped yelling curses, and thinking he had figured out a way to delay the performance, shouted earnestly, 'I want a preacher! You wouldn't deny a man a preacher, would you?'

The Vigilantes had thought of that, too, and had a preacher there. They knew, by this time, about all the tricks a man could think of to make a delay. Pete Gossard had nothing to say to the preacher, after all, except the frantic plea: 'Tell him to give me a good drop.'

'They will, Pete,' the preacher promised. He shivered and added, 'They always have. May God have mercy!'

There was still a lot of noise from the crowd of miners – the seven or eight hundred of them who had constituted the jury and had filed solemnly between two wagons to vote. Fourteen men had voted for acquittal, and after four hundred voted 'guilty', the Vigilantes had stopped the farce of tallying. The noise was far out on the edge of the crowd, where those who could not see clearly were milling around, but in the centre, at the hanging place, there was hardly any sound. Here death was, and the men who would beckon to it had nothing much to say.

The three packing boxes were sturdy; each had a rope tied to it by which it would be pulled away at the signal; the nooses were soundly wound. The Vigilantes, Wolfer Joe recollected, had had plenty of practice.

He felt a shudder coming over him, and to disguise it, he threw back his head and laughed.

He had few illusions about himself. Once he had said, grinning, 'Reckon I was born bad.' More accurately, he might have said, 'I was born outside the law, and mostly I've stayed outside it.' He had kept moving westward to places where the law was not. And what caught up with him at last was not law but anger. The angry men at the diggings could not wait for the law to catch up, they set up the Vigilance Committee to enforce ruthless justice.

Barney Gallagher frowned at that laugh. He stepped down from the box, wiping his hands on his pants, and said reflectively,'I was wondering – did you ever do one good thing in your life?'

Wolfer Joe looked into his eyes and answered with his lips pulled back from his teeth, 'Yeah. Once I betrayed a woman.'

At the hangman's signal, men pulled the ropes on the packing box.

The word love was in the language he used with women, but its meaning was not in his understanding when he met Annie. Even when he left her, he was not sure he knew the meaning, and after that he never had much chance to find out.

She stood with her arms outspread, her hands touching the barn wall, trembling, withdrawing not so much from Wolfer Joe as from life itself pressing toward her.

'You don't really like me,' he insisted. 'Bet you don't.'

'Maybe I do,' Annie answered, breathless. 'I got to go in now.' She could have ducked under his arm, but she only glanced up at him with a scared smile. She was seventeen years old. Wolfer Joe was twenty-nine.

'You go in now.' he said, 'and I'll know you don't love me.' He said the word lightly; he had said it before. The shape of it was easy in his mouth. 'I do so, I – love you,' she said. 'You could just as well stay here, instead of going on.'

Oh, no, not at twenty-nine. He could not stay in the settlements for long at a time. The law was creeping westward too fast. He was not sure what the law was, but he knew that he and his like had better keep ahead of it.

'Nothing here to keep me,' he said. The words hurt her as he had meant them to hurt, and she drew back. 'I got to go on,' he said. He added boldly, suddenly seeing a dream, 'Going to move on and settle down somewheres. Where I'm going, a girl like you wouldn't go. You wouldn't go with me.'

She was pressed tight against the barn wall. 'Maybe I would, if I wanted to.'

'Your pa wouldn't let you,' he scoffed.

'Pa couldn't stop me. Now let me be – let me go!' She struggled against him, but his arms were an iron cage, and his heart pounded against hers.

'Tonight at the fork of the trail,' he said when he let her go, when he loosed her arms from their clinging. 'Wait for me there – but you won't come.'

'I will,' she said. 'Because I, I – love you.'

That was the last thing she ever said to him.

'I believe you mean it,' he answered, and found his voice was hushed with wonder.'I guess you really do,' he said, trying to laugh.

The wonder was still on him when he waited where the trail forked. But Doubt hovered there too, and, roosting on his shoulder, Suspicion watched the trail with cold, yellow eyes.

If she came, he could take her west and build a soddy, get a bunch of cattle started – he knew how to swing a long loop on someone else's beef. He had done it before, for pay.

'What makes you think she'll come?' hooted Doubt, circling over him.

'What reason would she have if she did?' croaked Suspicion, with claws sharp in his shoulder.

'There's no reward out for me around here,' argued Wolfer Joe. 'Supposing she does come, her reason's her own business. It's her I want, not her reasons. I'll settle down somewheres. If she comes.'

He watched the trail from up above, belly down on a flat rock. He jerked when he saw her ride to the meeting place and look anxiously around. She had a little bundle of clothing tied to the saddle. He saw her dismount and look around again. But she didn't call out or say a word. She simply sat down to wait.

He was furious with an unreasoning anger. 'Damn little fool!' he whispered.

'Running off with a man she don't hardly know! What she'll get is no more'n she's got coming!'

He remembered that he himself was the man, and he lay there grinning at his own nonsense.

He would wait a while. When she gave up, he would appear and accuse her: 'I knowed it was just a notion. You never meant what you said. You start but you can't finish.'

Then he would let her go home weeping – or on with him, to do her crying later, when she knew what a fool she was.

But she did not give up. When darkness came, she built a little fire to keep the night away. With his heart pounding, with his lips pulled back from his teeth, Wolfer Joe lay on the flat rock, watching her. She had come so far, she had been so faithful. How long would she wait there for him? How far could he trust her?

Suspicion whispered, 'There'll come a day when she'll go crying to the law and say, "I know where Wolfer Joe is if you want him." '

He answered, 'You don't know my Annie.'

He watched her head bend forward on her knees as she waited and dozed. He saw it snap up again when a night sound scared her. After a while the fire burned low, and he knew she was sleeping. She awoke and fed it, and it blazed.

Then he knew he wasn't going down there. He saw not the girl, but her patience. He saw not the red glow of the fire, but faith abiding. He saw love by the fire, and he could not endure looking for fear he might see it end, during that night or some year to come.

He crept back off the rock and slid silently into the darkness to where his horse was waiting.

He lived for fourteen years after that. He was said to have seventeen notches on his gun, but that wasn't true. He never notched his gun butt for anything he did.

He was justly sentenced to hang for helping to murder two miners whom he and Pete Gossard and Knife Hilton had drygulched when the miners tried to take their gold out.

Wolfer Joe made an ending that earned him grim respect and he left Barney Gallagher puzzling about how betraying a woman could be a thing a man might boast of with the last words he ever had a chance to speak.

Dorothy M. Johnson

For Discussion

1   What is the difference between Kennedy's character and the characters of Gossard and Hilton?

2   What is a vigilante?

3   Discuss any other difficult or unusual words in the story.

4   At one point in the story, the storyteller moves backwards in time to tell of events that have taken place earlier. What is this called?

5   Why does Kennedy decide not to go with Annie?

THREE POEMS

The Walker of the Snow

Speed on, Speed on, good Master!
 The camp lies far away;
We must cross the haunted valley
 Before the close of day.

How the snow-blight came upon me
 I will tell you as we go,
The blight of the Shadow hunter
 Who walks the midnight snow.

To the cold December heaven
 Came the pale moon and the stars
As the yellow sun was sinking
 Behind the purple bars.

The snow was deeply drifted
 Upon the ridges drear
That lay for miles between me
 And the camp for which we steer.

'Twas silent on the hill-side
 And by the sombre wood
No sound of life or motion
 To break the solitude.

Save the wailing of the moose-bird
 With a plaintive note and low,
And the skating of the red leaf
 Upon the frozen snow.

And I said, "Though dark is falling,
 And far the camp must be,
Yet my heart it would be lightsome
 If I had but company."

And then I sang and shouted,
 Keeping measure as I sped,
To the harp-twang of the snow shoe
 As it sprang beneath my tread.

Not far into the valley
 Had I dipped upon my way,
When a dusky figure joined me,
 In a capuchon of gray,

Bending upon the snow-shoes
 With a long and limber stride;
And I hailed the dusky stranger,
 As we travelled side by side.

But no token of communion
 Gave he by word or look,
And the fear-chill fell upon me
 At the crossing of the brook.

For I saw by the sickly moonlight,
 As I followed, bending low,
That the walking of the stranger
 Left no foot-marks on the snow.

Then the fear-chill gathered o'er me
 Like a shroud around me cast,
And I sank upon the snow-drift
 Where the Shadow hunter passed.

And the Otter-trappers found me,
 Before the break of day.
With my dark hair blanched and whitened
 As the snow in which I lay.

But they spoke not, as they raised me,
 For they knew that in the night
I had seen the Shadow hunter,
 And had withered in his blight.

Sancta Maria speed us!
 The sun is falling low,
Before us lies the valley
 Of the Walker of the Snow!

Charles Dawson Shanly

For Discussion

1 What words and phrases in the first
 three verses build up a mood of
 suspense or horror?
2 What happens that finally terrifies
 the storyteller?
3 What happens at the end of the
 story?

Danny Deever

'What are the bugles blowin' for?' said Files-on-Parade.
'To turn you out, to turn you out,' the Colour-Sergeant said.
'What makes you look so white, so white?' said Files-on-Parade.
'I'm dreadin' what I've got to watch,' the Colour-Sergeant said.
   For they're hangin' Danny Deever, you can hear the Dead March play,
   The Regiment's in 'ollow square – they're hangin' him today;
   They've taken of his buttons off an' cut his stripes away,
   An' they're hangin' Danny Deever in the mornin'.

'What makes the rear-rank breathe so 'ard?' said Files-on-Parade.
'It's bitter cold, it's bitter cold,' the Colour-Sergeant said.
'What makes that front-rank man fall down?' said Files-on-Parade.
'A touch o' sun, a touch o' sun,' the Colour-Sergeant said.
   They're hangin' Danny Deever, they are marchin' of 'im round,
   They 'ave 'alted Danny Deever by 'is coffin on the ground;
   An' 'e'll swing in 'arf a minute for a sneakin' shootin' hound
   O they're hangin' Danny Deever in the mornin'!

"Is cot was right-'and cot to mine,' said Files-on-Parade.
"E's sleepin' out an' far tonight,' the Colour-Sergeant said.
'I've drunk 'is beer a score o' times,' said Files-on-Parade.
"E's drinkin' bitter beer alone,' the Colour-Sergeant said.
   They are hangin' Danny Deever, you must mark 'im to 'is place,
   For 'e shot a comrade sleepin' – you must look 'im in the face;
   Nine 'undred of 'is county an' the Regiment's disgrace,
   While they're hangin' Danny Deever in the mornin'.

'What's that so black agin the sun?' said Files-on-Parade.
'It's Danny fightin' 'ard for life,' the Colour-Sergeant said.
'What's that that whimpers over'ead?' said Files-on-Parade.
'It's Danny's soul that's passin' now,' the Colour-Sergeant said.
   For they're done with Danny Deever, you can 'ear the quickstep play,
   The Regiment's in column, an' they're marchin' us away;
   Ho! the young recruits are shakin', an' they'll want their beer today,
   After hangin' Danny Deever in the mornin'!

Rudyard Kipling

The Execution

On the night of the execution
a man at the door
mistook me for the coroner.
'Press,' I said.

But he didn't understand. He led me
into the wrong room
where the sheriff greeted me:
'You're late, Padre.'

'You're wrong,' I told him. 'I'm Press.'
'Yes, of course, Reverend Press.'
We went down a stairway.

'Ah, Mr Ellis,' said the Deputy.
'Press!' I shouted. But he shoved me
through a black curtain.
The lights were so bright
I couldn't see the faces
of the men sitting
opposite. But, thank God, I thought,
they can see me!

'Look!' I cried. 'Look at my face!
Doesn't anybody know me?'

Then a hood covered my head.
'Don't make it harder for us,'
      the hangman whispered.

Alden Nowlan

For Discussion

1. What words and phrases in the first verse of *Danny Dever* build up a mood of suspense or fear?
2. What has Danny Deever done?
3. How does the story end?
4. What story does *The Execution* tell?

CHRISTMAS IN THE TRENCHES

In this extract from Oh, What a Lovely War! *a group of British soldiers are in their trench at the front line. There are sounds of fighting not far away. It is Christmas, 1915. Suddenly they hear German soldiers singing 'Heilige Nacht' ('Silent Night') in their own trench on the other side.*

Characters

First Soldier
Second Soldier
Third Soldier
German Soldier

Fourth Soldier
Fifth Soldier
Sixth Soldier

Second Soldier (*as the Germans sing*) What is it?
Fifth Soldier Singing.
Third Soldier It's those Welsh bastards in the next trench.
Fifth Soldier It's Jerry that is.
First Soldier It's an 'ymn.

Sixth Soldier No – it's a carol.
Second Soldier Wouldn't have thought they had them.
Third Soldier It's Jerry all right, it's coming from over there.
Fourth Soldier Sings well for a bastard, doesn't he?
First Soldier Sing up, Jerry, let's hear you!
Fifth Soldier Put a sock in it, let's listen.

They listen as 'Heilige Nacht' finishes.

Second Soldier Nice, wasn't it? Good on you, mate!
German Soldier Hallo, Tommy! . . . Hallo, Tommy!
Fourth Soldier He heard you.

Second Soldier Hallo!

German Soldier Wie geht's?

First Soldier Eh?

German Soldier How are you, I am very well thank you, good night.

First Soldier That's another day gone!

German Soldier Hey, Tommy. How is it with you?

English Soldiers Lovely! Very good!

Third Soldier Guten Singing, Jerry!

Second Soldier Got any more?

German Soldier Fröhliche Weihnacht!

English Soldiers Eh?

German Soldier Good . . . Happy Christmas!

Second Soldier Happy Christmas!

First Soldier Hey! It's Christmas!

Fourth Soldier No. Tomorrow.

Second Soldier (*to first soldier*) What about opening your parcel?

First Soldier I forgot it was Christmas.

German Soldier Hallo, Tommy!

English Soldiers Yea?

German Soldier It is for you now to sing us a good song for Christmas, ja?

English Soldiers Oh, ja!

Third Soldier Let's give them one.

Second Soldier Go on then!

Third Soldier I can't sing.

First Soldier We know that.

Fourth Soldier Who's going to sing it, then?

Third Soldier (*to first*) Give them that one of yours.

First Soldier What – Cookhouse?

English Soldiers Yeah!!

First Soldier All right, Jerry, get down in your dugouts – it's coming over!

He sings 'Christmas Day in the Cookhouse'.

Sounds of Germans applauding: 'Bravo, Tommy.'

Fourth Soldier Hey, listen.

German Soldier Bravo, Tommy. English carols is very beautiful! Hey, Tommy, present for you, coming over!

English Soldiers Watch out! Get down!

The soldiers dive for cover. A boot is thrown from the darkness upstage and lands in the trench.

Third Soldier Quick, put a sandbag on it.

Sixth Soldier What is it?

Fifth Soldier It's a boot.

First Soldier Drop it in a bucket of water.

Fifth Soldier It's a Jerry boot.

Third Soldier What's that sticking out of it?

Sixth Soldier It's a bit of fir tree.

First Soldier A bit of ribbon.

Fifth Soldier Fags.

Fourth Soldier What's that?

Third Soldier That's chocolate, that is.

Second Soldier Is it?

Sixth Soldier Yeah.

English Soldier Thanks, Jerry!

First Soldier That's German sausage.

Second Soldier Is it?

First Soldier Yeah.

Second Soldier It's yours.

Fifth Soldier Eh, we'll have to send them something back, won't we?

Second Soldier Here, come on, get your parcel open.

First Soldier Here, what about your one, then?

Second Soldier Well, I ain't got one. Here, they can have my Christmas card from Princess Mary . . .

First Soldier Tell you what they can have, the old girl's Christmas pudding. Bet they've never tasted anything like that before. Here you are, I've been saving this. They can have my tin of cocoa – might help them sleep.

Fourth Soldier Nothing from me.

Fifth Soldier Right, Jerry, here's your Christmas box.

He throws the boot.

German Soldier Thanks, Tommy!

Explosion

First Soldier Blimey! The Christmas pudding wasn't that bad.

German Soldier Hey, Tommy! Are you still there?

English Soldiers Yeah! No thanks to you!

German Soldier Many greetings to you, for your many presents and kindnesses to us, we thank you.

**from *Oh, What a Lovely War!*
by Theatre Workshop**

For Discussion

1 What do the soldiers think is happening when the boot is thrown?

2 What do the English soldiers mean when they call back (at the end), 'Yeah! No thanks to you!'?

3 What is the first thing the German soldier does that shows he is friendly?

4 *Oh, What a Lovely War!* is a musical play. What other musicals have you seen – whether on stage or on film? What is the best one you have seen?

QUESTIONS *for work in pairs or small groups*

To answer these questions you will need to re-read all the texts in this Unit, and also to look at the pictures.

1 What is the first thing that Kennedy does in *The Last Boast* to show that he is not afraid?

2 Is this the first time the Vigilantes have hanged a man? How do you know?

3 Why does Kennedy decide not to go with Annie?

4 All three of the poems tell stories. Do these stories have anything in common?

5 In the scene from *Oh, What a Lovely War!* what presents do the Germans send with the boot?

6 What presents do the British soldiers send back?

7 In this scene, what do you think the writers are saying about the First World War?

Find and copy out *single words* from the texts that have these meanings:

8 a deep ditch (*Oh, What a Lovely War!*)

9 breathing noisily (*The Last Boast*, paragraph 7)

10 full of fear (*The Last Boast*, paragraph 8)

11 signal (*The Last Boast*, paragraph 10)

12 false ideas (*The Last Boast*, paragraph 13)

Finally look at the pictures in this Unit and choose one that you think could illustrate a story of your own. Write a synopsis (or short outline) of the story.

drawn for a radio play, Home Truths for Tony, *by Ed Briant*

LATER . . . *Read each other's synopses.*

Choose the most interesting one, and write a scene from a play based on your synopsis. Or write a short story or poem.

from GODAM directed by Dilip Chitre, 1984

2 The Paranormal

The paranormal is a controversial topic. Are there such things as telepathy, clairvoyance, and hypnosis? Or are they just the products of some people's imagination?

Woman with Head full of Cloud *by Salvador Dali*

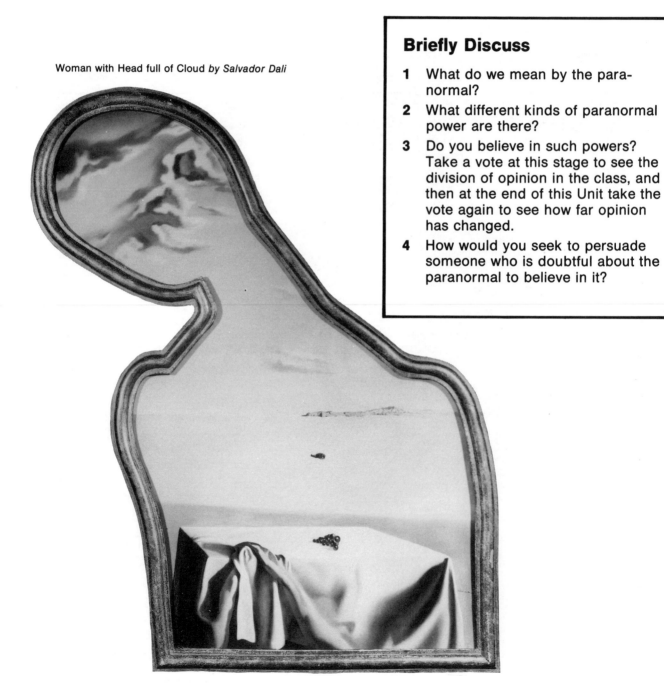

Briefly Discuss

1 What do we mean by the para-normal?

2 What different kinds of paranormal power are there?

3 Do you believe in such powers? Take a vote at this stage to see the division of opinion in the class, and then at the end of this Unit take the vote again to see how far opinion has changed.

4 How would you seek to persuade someone who is doubtful about the paranormal to believe in it?

Before you listen to the first passage, think again about the discussion of Question 2 above, making your own list of all the different kinds of paranormal power you can think of. Then as you listen to the passage, tick off all the powers mentioned by the writer that are also on your own list, and make a further list of the items you have omitted.

LISTENING COMPREHENSION

In Search of the Paranormal

1 Many people laugh when they hear talk of paranormal powers. They think it ridiculous that there are still things happening in the world that scientists cannot explain. They disapprove of the idea of minds being stronger and more powerful than bodies, or of messages travelling through time and space without the assistance of any known messengers. In fact, though, scientists have always been interested in things that they cannot at the moment explain, so, in laughing at the idea of the paranormal, we are really laughing at the very thing that has interested scientists over the centuries – the unknown, the unexplained, the inexplicable. Instead of telling people they are liars when they claim to have witnessed or performed paranormal feats, we should look into the evidence available and look around (if we accept some at least of the evidence) for good explanations.

2 The evidence, in fact, is all around us. Not only are newspapers and history books full of happenings and events, phenomena, occurrences, that cannot be simply explained, but such things occur frequently to each of us during our day to day lives. So I am not playing with words when I claim that the paranormal – the experience of something that cannot at first be explained or understood – does not itself happen abnormally, is not an unusual occurrence. In a sense, the paranormal is normal.

3 To illustrate my point, it will be helpful if I try to list some of the different kinds of paranormal experience that can occur. You can then put my theory to the test, simply by asking yourself – have you ever or often experienced any of these?

4 The commonest kind of paranormal experience occurs when somebody knows something in circumstances where, strictly speaking, he or she ought *not* to know. This is the case where you know that your best friend has had an accident *before* the fact itself is reported to you. This can take three different forms – clairvoyance, telepathy and precognition. *Clairvoyance* means that you know something without anyone telling you or trying to tell you, that you – as it were – see the information for yourself without knowing how you do it. Perhaps you call this intuition or instinct. In such cases, your mind is able to race across space more quickly than any motor car or aeroplane. You know what is happening a thousand miles away. You are, at that moment in time, clairvoyant.

5 *Telepathy* is slightly different. This means that you are able to pick up messages from someone else, even though neither of you knows how this is done. Somehow you

13

communicate without any apparent messages changing hands. This can happen between people who cannot see each other at the time, or indeed happen to be thousands of miles away from each other. One of them is able, as they say, to read the other's mind.

6 *Precognition* is a particular kind of clairvoyance in which someone picks up a message about a particular event *before* the event actually happens. People who have the gift of precognition to a high degree are called prophets or fortune tellers. Sometimes, of course, they are called witches or madmen.

7 Clairvoyance, telepathy and precognition are paranormal powers which all of us possess at some time or other. Sometimes these powers come to us while we are going about our daily lives. Sometimes they come to us while we sleep, in our dreams. But they do happen. They are not make-believe.

8 A second type or category of paranormal experience is concerned with the strange powers that some people have over others. The best example of this is *hypnosis*, in which one person (the hypnotist) appears to take control of the mind of his subject.

Under hypnosis we act not according to our own wishes but to the wishes of the hypnotist. Hypnosis is now used quite widely in doctors' surgeries and hospitals, instead of anaesthetics. Patients who respond to hypnosis do not need an anaesthetic before an operation, they only need the hypnotist to tell them they will feel no pain, and they feel no pain.

9 A third category is concerned with similar powers that some people can exercise over themselves. Perhaps the most famous of these is *levitation* – in which the person is able to float in the air. There have been many documented cases of such powers. Another form of such power is *firemastery*, in which a person is able to walk through a raging fire and emerge unharmed. Another form is *spontaneous human combustion*, or S.H.C. for short. This occurs when people suddenly catch fire without doing anything, and without anything being done to them. They simply burst into flames.

10 It is, finally, also possible for such powers to exist over things. In other words, some people can use the force of their minds to move things, make things and break things. The celebrated Uri Geller has been reported as making

a pair of cuff-links fly all on their own across the Atlantic when he discovered he had accidentally left them at home in his New York flat. The same gentleman has demonstrated many times on television programmes all over the world his ability to make spoons bend just by stroking them, and to make watches stop just by looking at them. The name given to such powers is *telekinesis* – meaning, to exert force over something without actually moving anything oneself.

11 These, then, are the main types of paranormal powers. I have deliberately left out of my discussion any mention of powers concerned with life and death. In other words, I have not talked about any kind of *contact with the dead*, such as the powers of a spiritualist to talk to dead persons. I have left these out of my discussion simply because I believe they raise different issues and different problems. Similarly, I have not talked about *U.F.O.s* and communications with outer space. And for the same reasons.

12 In effect, then, I have limited myself to paranormal experiences that occur every day in some form or another. It is now up to you. Am I right? Are these experiences common? If so, how do you think they are to be explained?

from *Science and the Inexplicable* by George McLaren

For Discussion

1 Which items does this writer consider which you did not yourself include?
2 Which items did you consider which this writer did not?
3 Is there any vocabulary here that you found difficult?
4 In general, does this writer feel that there is such a thing as the paranormal?
5 In general, does this writer make you want to rethink your views on the paranormal?

Multiple choice questions on

'In Search of the Paranormal'

In your notebooks write down the numbers 1 to 10 underneath each other, and then write down the letter of the best answer to each question.

1 The writer of the article thinks the paranormal is
  a) nonsense.
  b) an everyday happening.
  c) a very unusual and strange thing.

2 The word 'paranormal' is best defined as
  a) uncommon.
  b) weird.
  c) beyond any ordinary explanation.

3 'Clairvoyance' means
  a) knowing something without anybody telling you.
  b) knowing something that has not yet happened.
  c) knowing something without being sure about it.

4 Picking up messages from other people's minds is known as
  a) precognition.
  b) hypnotism.
  c) telepathy.

5 An anaesthetic
  a) puts you to sleep.
  b) makes you unable to feel pain.
  c) makes you feel very happy.

6 Which of these powers does the writer not deal with in this article?
  a) power to float on air
  b) power to set yourself on fire
  c) power to make contact with the dead

7 Under hypnosis we act
  a) according to our own wishes.
  b) according to the wishes of the hypnotist.
  c) according to the wishes of anyone who speaks to us.

8 'Levitation' means
  a) floating on air.
  b) the same as hypnosis.
  c) walking unharmed through fire.

9 The writer talks about a form of power called 'S.H.C.' which is short for 'spontaneous human combustion'. 'Combustion' means
  a) bursting into flames.
  b) blowing up.
  c) destroying.

10 'Telekinesis' means
  a) making something move without yourself using any force.
  b) making others use force without using any yourself.
  c) moving without using any force.

TELEPATHY – Fact or Fiction?

This is part of a magazine article about a Spanish lady who had a telepathic dream that saved the lives of herself and her friend.

Read the article together, working in pairs or small groups. Choose one word for each of the numbered spaces, choosing a word in each case that makes sense not only in the sentence but also in the article as a whole.

Just write out the numbers 1 to 20 underneath each other in your notebooks, and then write down the words at the side of them.

Early one morning in 1980 a very frightened old lady walked into a police station in Barcelona. Maria Isabella Casas was an 81-year-old widow. She had just had a terrible dream.

She told the officer on duty that she had seen the face of a friend and neighbour in her dream. The name of this friend and neighbour was Rafael Perez. In her dream he had twisted in terror and said, 'They are going to kill us!'

At first the police thought her story was just a –(**1**)–. But they became –(**2**)– when she told them she had not seen Perez for ten days. Normally he –(**3**)– to see her every day. This time he had written her a –(**4**)– saying he was going away for several weeks. Why had Perez not –(**5**)– to see her personally?

The police –(**6**)– to investigate and eventually they found Perez –(**7**)– up in a shed on the roof of the –(**8**)– of flats. He told them that two men had –(**9**)– into his apartment and made him –(**10**)– a large number of cheques so that they could –(**11**)– his life savings a little at a time. Then they –(**12**)– him to write the letter to Mrs Casas so that her –(**13**)– would not be aroused. Then they –(**14**)– him up and said they would be –(**15**)–. They said that when they returned and once they –(**16**)– all the money, they would kill him and his –(**17**)–. Astonishingly, the old –(**18**)– seems to have picked up the –(**19**)– of her friend as he waited in –(**20**)– for his captors to return. Her telepathic dream saved the lives of both of them.

from The Unexplained Volume 2

For Discussion

What further evidence do we need before we can accept this story as *proof* that telepathy does exist?

Read the whole extract through again before you decide finally on your answers.

SIXTH SENSE?

For Discussion

What do we mean by a sixth sense?
What different kinds of sixth sense are there?

Read the following magazine article.
The paragraphs are given here in the wrong sequence.
Working together in pairs or small goups, decide on the correct sequence.
Write out the numbers 1 to 6 underneath each other in your notebooks, and choose
the appropriate letter for each number. Re-read the whole passage in the order
which you think is right, before you finally decide on your answers.

In Search of the Sixth Sense

The human mind has powers of understanding that are beyond the reach of the five senses. As ROY STEMMAN shows, extrasensory perception is a fact – but one still shrouded in mystery.

A Thousands of people have had similar experiences. Somehow information reaches them in a way that bypasses their 'normal' senses. During the past 50 years investigators have used the term *extra-sensory perception* (ESP) to describe the phenomenon and hundreds of experiments have been conducted around the world in an attempt to confirm its existence scientifically and understand how it works.

B *Clairvoyance* It is just as likely that young Krippner had an awareness of his uncle's death – he sensed it had happened – without having any mind-to-mind communication.

Precognition Yet another possibility is that his knowledge came not from past or present events but from the future. Somehow he jumped fractionally ahead in time and knew what his mother was about to learn from the telephone call.

C What is clear from this research, and from a study of spontaneous cases, is that ESP is not an isolated phenomenon. Take Krippner's experience, for example. There are three 'psychic' ways, all classified as types of ESP, in which he might have found out about his uncle's unexpected death:

Telepathy It is possible that the teenager's mind 'tuned in' to his cousin's mind and read his thoughts just as he was about to telephone with the bad news.

D FOURTEEN-YEAR-OLD Stanley Krippner wanted an encyclopedia very badly. His parents had to refuse his request; they were apple farmers and a bad harvest had left them very short of money. Stanley went to his room and cried. After a while he began to think of ways of raising the money himself and his thoughts turned to his rich Uncle Max. How could he best approach him for funds?

E There is a fourth possibility: the dead uncle could have been communicating with his nephew. If that were the case, Krippner would have needed extra-sensory powers of *some* kind to be aware of the dead man's presence. Such communication is usually called mediumship and is outside the province of scientific research into ESP.

F Suddenly the teenager sat bolt upright in bed as a horrible thought flooded his mind: 'Uncle Max can't help me because he's dead.' Many years later, Krippner – now one of America's leading psychic investigators – recalled:

'At that moment I heard the telephone ring. My mother answered the phone, then began sobbing as my cousin told her that Max had unexpectedly taken ill, was rushed to hospital, and had just died.'

from *The Unexplained* Volume 1

For Discussion

Again, what further evidence do we need before we can accept this story?

PUNCTUATION: The Full Stop

The full stop is of course the most important mark of punctuation, separating one sentence from the next.

Briefly discuss – what is a sentence? How would you define it? Later, check the definition given in a dictionary.

Writing that leaves out or misuses the full stop tends either to have no meaning or to be very hard to follow. Take this example from a student's essay, and rewrite it with full stops and capital letters correctly used.

1 I have often wondered about the paranormal some people seem to believe that there definitely are such things as paranormal powers we discussed This in class and some of the students even said that they had Seen paranormal things happen.

After you have discussed your answers to the first example work on these on your own:

2 The trouble is that some people Exaggerate I am just not sure who to believe nothing paranormal has ever happened to me.

3 On one occasion my brother said he saw a ghost the trouble is that my brother is not very reliable for example He's easily scared he often thinks he hears things when I know that there's nothing there.

4 I believe in hypnotism I have known people who have been hypnotised my father was hypnotised once by the dentist because he cannot stand having any kind of injection.

5 So I don't think of hypnotism as strange or unusual I think it is really more normal than paranormal of course some people cannot be hypnotised for example my mother cannot be hypnotised she says that she cannot concentrate for long enough.

The Comma

The comma is second in importance to the full stop. The full stop marks a break *between* sentences, and the comma marks a slightly smaller or shorter break *in* the sentence. Like all marks of punctuation it is used simply *to help the reader to make sense of what he or she is reading*, and it tells the reader to pause slightly within the sentence.

Re-read 'In Search of the Sixth Sense' and note the number of times that the writer has used a comma. In each case, the comma helps the reader to make good sense of what is being read. In effect, it tells the reader to watch for slight changes of thought in the sentence instead of running one word into the next.

By way of example, read aloud each sentence where the writer of 'In Search of the Sixth Sense' has used a comma, and read it in two different ways:

 a) without a pause where the comma occurs, and   b) with a pause.

Now rewrite these sentences with commas used where you think they are necessary:

1 The paranormal baffles me but it does not worry me.

2 I think though I cannot be sure that I have some paranormal powers.

3 One day when the weather was extremely bad I decided to spend a quiet time at home.

4 It was a windy wet sort of day and everything in the house seemed to be rattling.

5 Suddenly moving from one room to another I had a strange sensation.

6 It's difficult to explain precisely what happened.

Note that you should only use commas when you think they are necessary to help the readers make sense of what they are reading.

The Riddle of Hypnosis

The next article looks at the connection between hypnotism and medicine. Before reading it, discuss:
1 What is hypnotism?   2 What is an anaesthetic?
3 Can hypnotism be used as an effective anaesthetic?
Now compare your own answers to the third question with the views of the writer of this article.

In one form or another, hypnotism has been with us throughout history. It has been used by witch doctors and even by priests in temples in ancient Greece. In modern times, hypnotism is known mostly because of the work of a European hypnotist called Franz Mesmer who lived from 1734 to 1815. His name has even become a word in the English language, for we talk of people mesmerising each other and of people being mesmerised.

Mesmer and his followers found out that some people are able to put others in a trance and that while they are in a trance they can be made to obey many commands. Also, in the course of their experiments they made two other important discoveries.

First, they found out that if someone was in a trance and was told, 'You will feel no pain', then he or she could be struck or pricked and even burned but would feel no pain. Then they showed that surgical operations could be performed on someone under hypnosis and the person would feel no pain. This was before anaesthetic drugs had been invented.

The medical profession refused to believe this. A man under hypnosis had his leg cut off and he felt no pain. But doctors said this was not possible.

Secondly, they found out that some people are more clever when they are hypnotised than they are normally. For example, some people can draw, others can sing. Many people refused to believe this but we now know that there is a lot of truth in what the Mesmerists said.

from *The Unexplained* Volume 2

After reading the article, write your answers to these questions:

1 Can hypnotism be used to anaesthetise patients? Copy out *one sentence* that most clearly shows how the writer of the article answers the question.

2 What is an anaesthetic?

3 Find and copy out another word from the article that means the same as *mesmerised*.

4 Find and copy out a word from the article that is the antonym (opposite) of *modern*.

5 Find and copy out a phrase from the article that is an antonym of *agreed*.

True or false?

For your answers to these questions just write down TRUE or FALSE. If you think a statement is TRUE, write down the number of the paragraph where you have found the answer.

6 The writer of this article thinks that some people are more clever when they are hypnotised than they are at other times.

7 The writer says that doctors did not at first want to believe in hypnotism as a way of stopping pain.

8 The writer says that hypnotism is the best kind of anaesthetic.

9 The writer says that there are times when hypnotism is of no use in operations.

10 The writer says that Franz Mesmer was a great doctor.

Now compare your answers with the rest of the class.

Who believes in the paranormal?

1 A Questionnaire

Work out a set of questions to put to the class, to establish students' attitudes towards the paranormal. Possible questions might include:

1 Has anything happened to you or to someone you know that makes you definitely believe in paranormal powers?

2 Do you think that most stories about the paranormal are true stories?

3 Do you think there should be more research into paranormal powers?

4 Would you yourself like to have paranormal powers?

First, discuss the questions, and make a note of any interesting experiences that are mentioned (perhaps when discussing Question **1** above).

Then put the questions to the vote and make a note of the voting. Keep your notes for use later.

2 Fair and Unfair Arguments

In discussing questions about the paranormal it is possible to use many different arguments. As in any argument it is also possible to use fair and unfair methods of arguing. In other words, it is possible to cheat.

Some of the most widely used kinds of cheating are:

a) saying things that are so vague and generalised that nobody can possibly prove or disprove them.

An example would be:
There are many more cases nowadays of the paranormal than you might think.

b) saying that there is evidence to back up what you have said, but not giving the evidence.

An example would be:
There was a case in London in 1985 in which a Frenchman showed he had telekinetic powers by making his watch fly across the English Channel. (No details are given, so nobody can check whether this happened.)

Working in pairs or small groups, answer the following questions about the articles you have read in this Unit. For each answer you should copy out just one sentence.

1 Find and copy out an example of **a)** in the first three paragraphs of 'In Search of the Paranormal'.

2 Find and copy out an example of **a)** in paragraph 7 of the same article.

3 Find and copy out an example of **b)** in paragraph 10 of the same article.

4 Find and copy out an example of **a)** in 'In Search of the Sixth Sense'.

5 Find and copy out an example of **b)** in the same article.

6 Find and copy out an example of **a)** in 'The Riddle of Hypnosis'.

7 Find and copy out an example of **b)** in the same article.

8 Make up a sentence of your own about telepathy, as an example of **a)**.

9 Make up a sentence of your own about clairvoyance, as an example of **b)**.

10 Make up a sentence of your own about telekinesis, as an example of **a)**.

3 Essay Writing

Write an essay on the paranormal, in which you answer and also discuss this question:

Do you believe in the paranormal?

Before you begin writing, talk about ways in which you might plan your essay.

A possible plan would be:

1 Explain what the paranormal is, giving the names of different kinds of paranormal powers.

2 Tell some stories about different kinds of paranormal powers. Some of these might come from class discussion, some might come from the articles in this Unit or from your own research in the library.

3 Give your own views on the stories, explaining whether you believe them and why.

4 Give the views of the rest of the students as shown in their answers to the questionnaire.

5 Sum up your own views.

Note: In your writing, be as fair as you can, and try always to give more than one point of view.

Use phrases and words such as *however, on the other hand, but*, and *perhaps*.

Assessing your Essays

Later, talk about ways of assessing your essays.

A possible way of assessment would be to look especially at:

a) whether the essay has clearly followed a good plan;

b) whether the essay is fair to different points of view;

c) whether phrases and words such as *however, on the other hand*, and *but* have been used;

d) whether the writer has drawn on a variety of experiences, including some of his or her own as well as some from books and articles and from other people;

e) punctuation, especially the use of full stops and commas.

Write a short assessment of your own essay.

Read one or two of each other's essays and, without seeing the other readers' assessments, write your own. Later, compare your assessments.

The Yellow Book

An Illustrated Quarterly

Volume III October 1894

Price
$1.50
Net

London: John Lane
Boston: Copeland & Day

Price
5/-
Net

3 Episodes

Most of the stories in this Unit are taken from novels or from long 'short' stories. Listen to the first one, talk about it, and then read the others.

GOODBYE, ILHA!

You are so punctual, Ilha, I know you will be here exactly one hour after dawn, as we arranged yesterday. I am leaving this letter to explain why I cannot meet you. You must report to World Resource headquarters. Be quick. Roll to the place we left the skid-plane; fly with throttle wide open; you should arrive before noon.

Claim emergency; get an immediate interview with the Director.

Before the afternoon is over he is to blanket the whole area, quad 73:61 on the map, with infrared heat. Not to kill, tell him. Raise the absolute temperature only about 10 per cent, just enough to make it thoroughly uncomfortable. These visitors endanger our whole civilization, but I think that will drive them away. However, it may not, so at noon the *next* day push the power up to full killing temperatures for a few minutes.

He will object, but what if a few miles of sand are fused? You know the area. It was so thoroughly blasted during the Age of Wars that no more damage is possible, and anyway, it will be centuries before the reclamation engineers touch this part of our planet. You can – you *must* persuade him, Ilha!

It is rude, I know, to begin with such urgency, omitting the traditional greeting phrases, writing without Limik calmness or philosophy. But you may as well get used to it, for the creatures I write about are totally un-Limik – utterly out of this world!

I found them yesterday about where the disturbance showed on the magnetic map, near the center of the quad. Their rocket ship is much like the ancient ones in the museum at Prr, but larger and made of magnesium. I hid behind a sand dune until dark, when I could examine it safely. Light streamed from two round windows and also from a tall, narrow, opening – a door in spite of its fantastic shape (twice as high as it was broad) – opening from a small vestibule. There were two inner doors, one open and one closed. From the closed one came loud roarings and barkings as of wild animals, but modulated by a variety of smacks, gargles and splutterings. I soon realized these sounds were signals – a regular code language, like our own writing. I could sense the thought associated with each sound; but evidently the animals behind the door, though all present together, could not. They had to make these sound signals to understand each other. Curious and primitive, isn't it?

There were three voices, one much stronger than the other two. I caught thought phrases like 'I am hungry,' 'Is not that drink cold yet?' and 'When do we eat?' There were thoughts I sensed, which made no meaning to me. There were also sounds, many of them, that had no thought behind them at all: 'WEL-IL-BEDAM' was one, 'OG-O-AWN' was another, commonest of all was a sort of barking, 'HAW-HAW-HAW'. All meaning dissolved when they barked, their minds seemed pleased with themselves in a strange, bubbling, thought-free sort of way. 'HAW HAW HAW' would go the biggest voice and the other two (no, not its mates; I still know nothing of their reproductive customs except that the wrappings on their bodies have something to do with it) would join 'HAW HAW

HAW' like so many flepas barking at the moon. Only flepas think sad hungry thoughts when they bark; these creatures stopped thinking altogether.

I stood there outside the door delighted with it. I suppose it doesn't sound attractive – though I ask you, can any Limik stop thinking – ever? But it is more than not thinking. It is the feeling that goes with it – a lifting of the spirits, refreshing, youthful . . . Oh well, I'll continue.

The open door showed a small empty room, its walls fitted with shelves and cabinets. I tip-probed in, hoping to learn something about this unknown species from its environment. A repulsive odor came from a bowl on the long shelf and I climbed up – burning myself, incidentally, for all that part of the shelf was hot. What do you suppose was in that bowl? Pieces torn from the bodies of living vegetables and animals, all stewing together in a revolting mixture. Their food! Our savage ancestors might have enjoyed it; I was filled with horror and retreated along the shelf to the other end of the room. Here stood a smaller metal bowl, icy cold, smelling like our own poggle fuit. You know me and poggles! I think the brightest page in Limik history is our treaty with the poggle-people – we enjoy the fruit, they have their seeds better distributed. The odor from this bowl was irresistible, contrasted with the gruesome stench from the other end of the room. I dipped in my courtesy probe and drank.

It was not poggle juice, but some strange poison!

I wooshed, too late. My probe tip began to swell and throb; my fore-eye rolled so dizzily I had to somersault tail-over-feeler, putting my crippled probe in tail position. Even then I could not stand up, but fell several times. I thought I was going to die . . . While I tumbled about on that shelf I knocked over a pile of plates. They fell to the floor with an enormous crash, and an instant later the closed door burst open and three amazing monsters thundered into the room.

They were about six probes high, scarcely one wide – weird, attenuated and huge. They had five probes. Two were feelers, or perhaps tails, kept covered (they call them 'LAIGS'). Two were courtesy probes ('HANS') uncovered at the tips, which have no openings . . . but are each slit into five small tentacles. The fifth probe was short, stubby, and has no counterpart in Limik anatomy. It ends in a great bristle of hairs; two of the monsters had brown hairs, one red. All had one huge opening set with even, white pieces of bone – a little like a grinding machine. Two eyes were in each of these probes (migrated here from the body? I don't know. Our old bio professor would be interested. There may be residual eyes left on the body, too. They keep them tightly wrapped so there is no way to find out).

They strode with enormous steps – *sideways*, not probe after probe like our amble – and swayed awkwardly as they came. I remember thinking that our own wheel-like rolling would out-distance them, if I could ever get a free start. But they stood between me and the door. I was caught. The whole room rolled and turned before my eyes.

from *Goodbye, Ilha!* by Lawrence Manning

For Discussion

1 Who or what is telling the story?
2 Where is the story taking place?
3 Who are the creatures the storyteller is describing in the rocket ship?
4 What is happening at the end of this extract?
5 What may happen next?
6 What kind or genre of story is this?

Captured by the Redcoats

Charlie is only a boy, but he and his friends are fighting with the Maroons against the English soldiers who have come to make slaves of his people. In this part of the story, his friends have stolen the muskets off a group of soldiers, and Charlie has been caught.

'All right, you come along with me,' said the fat soldier, after Charlie had stopped struggling.

Gripping the boy's arm tightly, he pushed him ahead, forcing him to trip forward on his toes.

'Where did those boys suddenly come from?' said the fat soldier to his companion.

The tall one shook his head, his face still twisted with pain.

'Don't know. They must have been hiding in the bush. I suddenly saw them running towards our muskets. I grabbed at them but they had some greasy stuff on their skins and slipped from my hands. Then one of them struck my ankle.'

'Is it broken?'

'I don't think so, but it's in bad shape.' He looked angrily up at his comrade. 'If you had not been so greedy for meat, this would not have happened.'

'No need to yell at me. We at least caught one of them.'

As the tall soldier looked at him, Charlie felt smaller than a beetle.

He was terribly afraid. He was sure that they would show him no mercy.

'Get me a stone so I can break every bone in his body,' said the tall man.

'No, we won't kill him yet. The captain will want to talk to him. He can lead us to the Maroon village.'

Charlie began to sob. He could not help it. His arm felt as if it was being torn from his body.

'Then tie him up, and help me with my leg,' the tall one growled.

Charlie's arms were tied behind him by the leather strap from the water-bottle of one of the soldiers. Afterwards he was thrown to the ground.

The tall soldier still seemed to be in pain. He took off his boot, exposing a badly swollen ankle. He groaned as his comrade bandaged it with strips of cloth torn from his shirt. Both men continued to talk in angry tones. They swore about what they would do to Charlie when they returned with him to their camp. The boy, hearing this,

tried to crawl away. With a swing of his hand, the tall soldier struck Charlie a hard blow on the mouth.

The boy cried out. His mouth started to bleed and a tooth was loosened.

'You try that again and I will knock you down,' the Redcoat bellowed.

They made their way back to camp, pushing Charlie ahead of them. The Maroon boy knew that, even if he made a dash into the forest, he could not run very fast with his arms lashed behind him.

They went past the Redcoat sentry and were greeted with shouts as the soldiers saw them. Charlie was taken into the presence of the captain. He stood with his head down while the two Redcoats explained what had happened.

'I should have you both court-martialled for allowing a couple of Maroon boys to get the better of you,' the captain, a stout, red-haired man with a fierce moustache, said angrily.

Turning to Charlie, he asked in a

thundering voice, 'Where were you going, boy?'

'No-no-nowhere, sir,' stammered Charlie, frightened almost out of his wits.

'You are lying!' shouted the captain.

The captain put his hand on the hilt of his sword. Charlie thought that the fierce man was about to draw it and plunge it into him. His knees began to knock together.

'To-to-hunt – we were going on a hunt!' he cried out.

The captain looked at him without saying a word. Then he shook his head.

'You are lying. No Maroon would be hunting around these parts knowing that we were up in the mountains. There was something peculiar about that attack this morning. The Maroons were trying to pull us away from here. They did not want to fight, but just to have us follow them. Why did they want to lead us away from here?' he roared.

Charlie was dumb. To the boy the captain seemed like an angry giant, ready to eat him up.

'Was it to get you boys past us? Was that it? Have the Maroons sent for help?' roared the giant.

Charlie was too terrified to reply. He wished he could shrink into the ground. He wanted to run away but the hated Redcoats were all around him. The brass buttons on their chests hurt his eyes. He could smell the leather they wore and see their big, red faces turned towards him.

The captain brought his face closer to Charlie's.

'We shall soon loosen your tongue,' he said in a terrible whisper.

With his eyes still fixed on Charlie's he snapped a finger at one of his soldiers.

'Soldier, build me a fire and heat some irons red hot. We will warm the roots of his tongue and see if that will make him talk,' he said.

Charlie whimpered. His knees gave way and he fell to the ground.

'Hurry up with that fire!' the captain shouted savagely as he began to unbuckle his sword.

from *The Young Warriors* by V. S. Reid

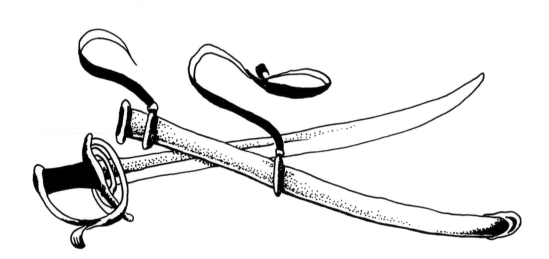

For Discussion

1   From what you can tell from this extract, how have the boys managed to get the soldiers' muskets?
2   Whose side are you on – the boys' or the soldiers'?
3   Whose side does the writer want you to be on?
4   What do you think will happen next?
5   What genre of story is this?

IMAMU

This is the opening of a novel set in Harlem, New York.

It was almost dawn when Imamu opened his eyes and lay staring through the darkness. He was fully dressed. He put his hands out to feel the sides of his bunk, but they kept reaching out until they touched the edges of a bed. The room was stuffy – the familiar stuffiness, a mixture of decay and stale wine. He was not at the detention centre; he was at home.

He sat up, swung his feet to the floor, and listened. He had fallen asleep waiting for his mother. Had she come in? He got up to move towards the door and stumbled, falling back on the bed. He switched on the light and saw the duffel bag he had packed with his clean clothes in his room last night. The rest of his clothes lay scattered over the untidy room, where he had left them a month earlier, before he went to the detention centre. He sure wasn't leaving much behind.

He inspected the room, as though seeing it for the first time. Most of the plaster had fallen off the walls, leaving the wooden boards exposed. The window shades had been pulled from their rollers and lay crumpled on the floor. The grey morning hulked outside the windows as though dreading to enter the room. A movement caught his eye, and he turned quickly – cockroaches were scurrying to hide beneath the worn linoleum. The sheets on his bed had turned a dark grey and would remain that way until he stole more to replace them. It would be the same in his mother's room.

Leaving the bedroom, he went to her room in the front. The wall switch did not work, so he made his way to the lamp on the night table near her bed, stumbling over empty wine bottles as he went. When he turned on the light, he saw the twisted disorder of the empty bed. Disappointed at not finding her there, he reached into his shirt pocket for a toothpick. He placed it between his teeth and worked it from one corner of his mouth to the other. He had not expected her, but even so, her absence shafted him with pain.

27

He sat on the edge of her bed, wishing her to come home. Wishing, because he wanted no part of the scenes that came with going out to find her and dragging her home. He had never been able to stop himself. When he found her drinking on the corner or on the avenue islands with her wino friends, anger took over. He would shout at her, 'Get up. Come on, get the hell on up.' Then he'd drag her away. It didn't matter if she wanted to come with him or not.

What rights did he have? None. She had taken away his rights when she had not come to jail to see him. It was over a month since he had been picked up with Iggy and Muhammed at the grocery store . . . She had to have heard about it. Someone must have told her. But she hadn't shown her face. Not at the detention centre, not in the court. One month! That sure had taken away his rights.

Yet he kept sifting through his mind all of the places she might be. Hard to say. Winos usually hung around the same places, except when a new member staggered into their scene. Then they could be anywhere in the city – sometimes even out of the city. The trouble between Imamu and his mother was that he tried to keep her in the neighbourhood – more precisely, in the house. He kept after her, forced her to leave her buddies, forced her to get sleep. The problem with that was that he was never willing to stay home for long with her. He had to go out. And so she kept going out and he had to keep after her. Well, she had had her way. For one month she had had her way.

Imamu took the cracked toothpick from his mouth and threw it on to the floor. He went to the bathroom, took off his sneakers, searched until he found his shoe whitener, and covered up the grey sneakers with the brilliant white polish. Then he washed, using toilet paper to dry himself because the towels were stiff with dirt. He scrubbed and polished his teeth with more toilet paper, then went into his room, put on a fresh shirt and transferred his toothpicks from the pocket of the dirty shirt to the clean one. He was ready. But for what?

from *The Disappearance* by Rosa Guy

For Discussion

1 What different things do you learn from this extract about Imamu's mother?
2 What do you learn about Imamu himself?
3 What do you think will happen next?
4 What genre of story do you think this is?

PUNCTUATION: The Comma

In the last Unit, it was explained that *in general* the comma is used to tell the reader to pause slightly in the reading of a sentence.

There are also *particular cases* where commas are *always* used. These include:

    a) marking off the items in a list.
    b) (with speech marks) marking off what is said.

a) Items in a list

Examples of this would be: She studied history, physics, chemistry and engineering.

He was known to be kindly, patient, polite and friendly.

You can look for gold, you can hunt for silver, you can dream of a fortune, but you still have to work for a living.

Find an example of this use of commas in the final paragraph of *Imamu*.

b) With speech marks

Notice the way the conversation is set out in *Captured by the Redcoats.*
Notice in particular the uses of **speech marks, capital letters,** and **commas.**

For example, how would you punctuate these sentences?

He said *I am going home.*

I am going he said.

I am going home he said *before it is too late.*

In each of these sentences the words in italics are the words that have actually been spoken.

Note In *Captured by the Redcoats*, the writer has changed to a new line, half a centimetre or so in from the margin, every time another person speaks.

Working on your own, rewrite the following conversation with any necessary punctuation. Perhaps break in the middle of the exercise to discuss your answers before finishing the exercise.

> He said i will come with you.
> I can find my own way home she said.
> But it's very late, John insisted.
> If I hurry she said I can still catch the last bus.
> I will come with you to the bus stop John said.
> Kate replied I'm used to looking after myself. You don't have to look after me.
> There was a pause and then John said you seem angry about something.
> There's nothing for me to be angry about said Kate.
> We've had a pleasant evening John said but now you're angry with me.
> You're imagining things said Kate and walked away.

FILM GENRES

Most (but not all) stories can be said to belong to different genres. This is true not only of novels but also of films.

What genres would you say are represented by the stills below? They are all taken from popular films.

1

2

3

Discuss them in groups, and:

- see if you can agree on the genre of each one.
- name two or three films you have seen that belong to the genre.
- name a couple of authors and/or novels that belong to the genre.

30

Later, still in groups, make a list of any genres that are not represented in this collection of stills.

Name two or three films and two or three novels or novelists that represent each genre.

Now compare your answers with the rest of the class.

31

BUTTERFLIES AND MOTHBALLS

Joan is thirteen and goes for dancing lessons after school, and she is looking forward to the end of term show. She is to take part as a butterfly in a dance devised by the teacher. She likes her costume though she is a little afraid that she looks too big and perhaps slightly ridiculous. But nothing can spoil the excitement of getting ready for the dress rehearsal until Miss Flegg, the dance teacher, takes her to one side.

She leaned down, placed her hand on my round bare shoulder, and drew me over to a corner. There she knelt down and gazed with her forceful black eyes into mine. Her blurred eyebrows rose and fell.

'Joan, dear,' she said, 'how would you like to be something special?'

I smiled at her uncertainly.

'Would you do something for me, dear?' she said, warmly.

I nodded. I liked to help.

'I've decided to change the dance a little,' she said. 'I've decided to add a new part to it; and because you're the brightest girl in the class, I've chosen you to be the special, new person. Do you think you can do that, dear?'

I had seen enough of her to know that this kindness was suspect, but I fell for it anyway. I nodded emphatically, thrilled to have been selected. Maybe I'd been picked to do the butterfly duet with Roger, maybe I would get bigger, more important wings. I was eager.

'Good,' said Miss Flegg, clamping her hand on my arm. 'Now come and hop into your new costume.'

'What am I going to be?' I asked as she led me away.

'A mothball, dear,' she answered serenely, as if this were the most natural thing in the world . . .

I was wounded when it turned out that Miss Flegg wanted me to remove my cloudy skirt and spangles and put on one of the white teddy-bear costumes the Tensies were using for their number,

'Teddy Bears' Picnic'. She also wanted me to hang around my neck a large sign that said MOTHBALL, 'So they'll all understand, dear, what you're supposed to be.' She herself would make the sign for me, in the interval between the rehearsal and the performance.

'Can I wear my wings?' I asked . . .

'Now, who ever heard of a mothball with wings?' she said in what was supposed to be a jocular but practical manner.

Her idea was that once the butterflies had finished their cavorting, I would lumber in among them in the white suit and the sign, and the butterflies would be coached to scatter. It would be cute, she told me.

'I liked the dance the way it was,' I said. 'I want it to be the way it was.' I was on the verge of crying; probably I had already begun.

Miss Flegg's manner changed. She put her face down close to mine so I could see the wrinkles around her eyes up close and smell the sour toothpaste smell of her mouth, and said, slowly and distinctly, 'You'll do as I say or you won't be in the dance at all. Do you understand?'

Being left out altogether was too much for me. I capitulated, but I paid for it. I had to stand in the mothball suit with Miss Flegg's hand on my shoulder while she explained to the other Teenies, sylphlike in their wispy skirts and shining wings, about the change in plans and my new, starring role. They looked at me, scorn on their painted lips; they were not taken in . . .

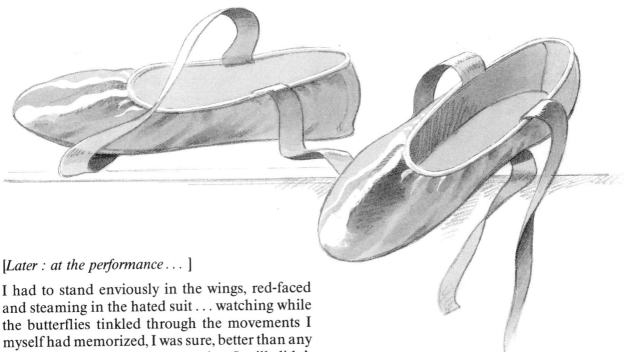

[*Later : at the performance . . .*]

I had to stand enviously in the wings, red-faced and steaming in the hated suit . . . watching while the butterflies tinkled through the movements I myself had memorized, I was sure, better than any of them. The worst thing was that I still didn't understand quite why this was being done to me, this humiliation disguised as a privilege.

At the right moment Miss Flegg gave me a shove and I lurched onto the stage, trying to look, as she had instructed me, as much like a mothball as possible. Then I danced. There were no steps to my dance, as I hadn't been taught any, so I made it up as I went along. I swung my arms, I bumped into the butterflies, I spun in circles and stamped my feet as hard as I could on the boards of the flimsy stage, until it shook. I threw myself into the part, it was a dance of rage and destruction, tears rolled down my cheeks behind the fur, the butterflies would die; my feet hurt for days afterwards. 'This isn't me,' I kept saying to myself, 'they're making me do it'. Yet even though I was concealed in the teddy-bear suit, which flopped about me and made me sweat, I felt naked and exposed, as if this ridiculous dance was the truth about me and everyone could see it.

The butterflies scampered away on cue and much to my surprise I was left in the center of the stage, facing an audience that was not only laughing but applauding vigorously. Even when the beauties, the tiny thin ones, trooped back for their curtsey, the laughter and clapping went on, and several people, who must have been fathers rather than mothers, shouted 'Bravo mothball!' It puzzled me that some of them seemed to like my ugly, bulky suit better than the pretty ones of the others.

After the recital Miss Flegg was congratulated on her priceless touch with the mothball. Even my mother appeared pleased. 'You did fine,' she said, but I still cried that night over my thwarted wings. I would never get a chance to use them now, since I had decided already that much as I loved dancing school I was not going back to it. It's true I had received more individual attention than the others, but I wasn't sure it was a kind I liked. Besides, who would think of marrying a mothball?

from *Lady Oracle* by Margaret Atwood

For Discussion

1 Why does Miss Flegg change Joan's role in the dance?

2 Why is Joan so hurt at the change of plans?

3 Why does she feel so hurt even after the audience have cheered her?

4 She says, 'I capitulated'. What does this mean?

5 This extract comes from the beginning of the novel. What is the rest of the novel likely to be about?

THREE POEMS *These three poems all tell stories.*

Lessons

I saw you in the street today.
You at your bus-stop,
Me at mine.
Facing each other.
Separated by a small stretch of tarmac.
Or was it more than that?
Memories of the childish pranks
Encouraged by your bets and dares.
We led you on,

Yet you led us.
I never knew which
For sure.
Our eyes meet at last
Amidst the crowd.
I wait for recognition.
I saw you in the street today.
You did not know me.

Lorraine Grant (17)

The Combat

It was not meant for human eyes,
That combat on the shabby patch
Of clods and trampled turf that lies
Somewhere beneath the sodden skies
For eye of toad or adder to catch.

And having seen it I accuse
The crested animal in his pride,
Arrayed in all the royal hues
Which hide the claws he well can use
To tear the heart out of the side.

Body of leopard, eagle's head
And whetted beak, and lion's mane,
And frost-grey hedge of feathers spread
Behind – he seemed of all things bred.
I shall not see his like again.

As for his enemy, there came in
A soft round beast as brown as clay;
All rent and patched his wretched skin;
A battered bag he might have been,
Some old used thing to throw away.

Yet he awaited face to face
The furious beast and the swift attack.
Soon over and done. That was no place
Or time for chivalry or for grace.
The fury had him on his back.

And two small paws like hands flew out
To right and left as the trees stood by.
One would have said beyond a doubt
This was the very end of the bout,
But that the creature would not die.

For ere the death-stroke he was gone,
Writhed, whirled, huddled into his den,
Safe somehow there. The fight was done,
And he had lost who had all but won.
But oh his deadly fury then.

A while the place lay blank, forlorn,
Drowsing as in relief from pain.
The cricket chirped, the grating thorn
Stirred, and a little sound was born.
The champions took their posts again.

And all began. The stealthy paw
Slashed out and in. Could nothing save
These rags and tatters from the claw?
Nothing. And yet I never saw
A beast so helpless and so brave.

And now, while the trees stand watching, still
The unequal battle rages there,
And the killing beast that cannot kill
Swells and swells in his fury till
You'd almost think it was despair.

Edwin Muir

34

The Rime of the Ancient Mariner

A sailor kills an albatross that is following his ship. The crew later decide that by killing the bird he has brought a great curse on the ship . . .

Down dropt the breeze, the sails dropt down,
'Twas sad as sad could be;
And we did speak only to break
The silence of the sea!

All in a hot and copper sky,
The bloody Sun, at noon,
Right up above the mast did stand,
No bigger than the Moon.

Day after day, day after day,
We stuck, nor breath nor motion;
As idle as a painted ship
Upon a painted ocean.

Water, water, every where,
And all the boards did shrink;
Water, water, every where,
Nor any drop to drink.

The very deep did rot: O Christ!
That ever this should be!
Yea, slimy things did crawl with legs
Upon the slimy sea.

About, about, in reel and rout
The death-fires danced at night;
The water, like a witch's oils,
Burnt green, and blue and white.

And some in dreams assurèd were
Of the Spirit that plagued us so;
Nine fathom deep he had followed us
From the land of mist and snow.

And every tongue, through utter drought,
Was withered at the root;
We could not speak, no more than if
We had been choked with soot.

Ah! well a-day! what evil looks
Had I from old and young!
Instead of the cross, the Albatross
About my neck was hung.

Samuel Taylor Coleridge (extract)

For Discussion

1 What story does 'Lessons' tell?
2 What story does 'The Combat' tell?
3 Choose a phrase from the last poem that most vividly shows the stillness of the ship in the middle of the ocean.
4 Which of the poems do you think paints the clearest and most powerful picture? Read them again before you decide.

QUESTIONS *for individual work*

*Work on these questions on your own, re-reading all the four
extracts from the novels or short stories in this Unit.*

Goodbye, Ilha!

1   Who are the aliens in the rocket ship?

2   What is the name of the type of creature living on this planet?

3   The writer says that the monsters in the ship have 'five probes'. What are the five probes?

4   What do we learn from this extract about:
    a) the appearance of the creatures who live on this planet? and
    b) the way they move?

Captured by the Redcoats

5   Write out the first sentence in the extract that clearly shows that the Redcoats mean to kill Charlie eventually.

6   Why does Charlie not attempt to escape when the soldiers are taking him back to their camp?

7   What does the captain think Charlie and his friends are actually trying to do?

Imamu

8   Copy out the first sentence in the extract that clearly shows that Imamu has been in trouble with the police.

9   What has he been in trouble for?

10 What is it that most upsets him about his mother?

Butterflies and Mothballs

11 Copy out the first sentence in the extract that shows clearly that Miss Flegg has no intention of changing her mind.

12 Why is Joan upset even after the performance, and after she has been such a success?

13 Does Joan have any friends at the dancing school? Explain how you can tell.

Vocabulary

14 Find and copy out a word in the third paragraph of *Goodbye, Ilha!* that means *put at risk*.

15 Find and copy out a word in the same paragraph that means the opposite of *barbarism or savagery*.

16 In the last sentence of *Captured by the Redcoats*, the captain *unbuckled* his sword. The prefix *un* is used here to mean that the action of buckling is reversed. Other examples would be:

    cover - uncover
    tangle - untangle

In front of which of these words can the same prefix be used? Write them out with the prefix in front of them if that makes a new word:

    build, ravel, clasp, wrap, block

(For example, if you can *unbuild* something you will write 'unbuild' as part of your answer. Otherwise, you will leave it and go on to the next word.)

17 In the last sentence but one of *Imamu*, he 'transferred' his toothpicks. The prefix *trans* is used in front of many words to mean *across*. For example, *transferred* means *changed across from one to the other*.

    Make a list of four other words using the same prefix.

18 Find and copy out one word from the last paragraph of *Butterflies and Mothballs* that means *frustrated* or *defeated*.

Genres

19 Name a couple of genres of stories that you enjoy reading (or that you enjoy watching on film).

20 Name
    a) a couple of novels that you have very much enjoyed reading, and
    b) a couple of novels that you have heard of and think you would enjoy reading.

USING THE LIBRARY

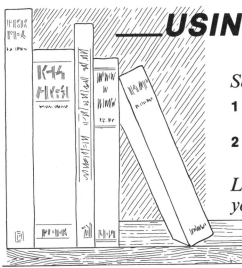

See if you can borrow from the library:

1 a novel you have not yet read of a genre that you know you like, and
2 a novel of a quite different genre, perhaps one that you do not normally read.

Later, talk about the novels and discuss whether or not you think your taste is changing.

WRITING

Write a chapter for any novel you would like to read.

Note: *The chapter does not have to be the first. It can come from any part of the story.*

Later, perhaps, write another chapter. Then read each other's chapters.

The British Library Reading Room

4 Rights

The various sections in this Unit are designed to test your knowledge of your own legal rights.

Working in pairs or small groups, discuss your answers to each section, and later compare your answers with those of the rest of the class.

Write down the numbers 1 to 24, and beside each write the age that you think is the correct answer.

The Law Says You Can . . .

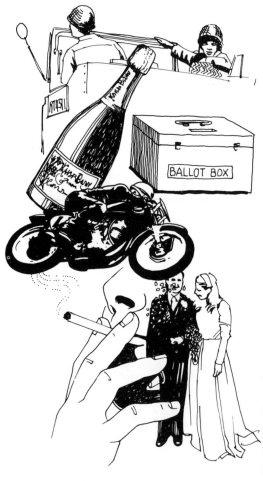

1	*vote* at . . . .
2	*smoke* in public and buy cigarettes at . . . .
3	*drink* alcohol in a pub at . . . .
4	*drink* beer or cider with a meal in a pub at . . . .
5	*drink* soft drinks in a pub at . . . .
6	*work* part-time (but your boss may need a permit) at
7	*claim* social security at . . . .
8	*join* the Army, Navy or Air Force at . . . .
9	*join* the Women's Army, Navy or Air Force at . . . . . .
10	*drive* a moped at . . . .
	a car or motorbike at . . . .
	a bus or lorry at . . . .
11	*get married* at . . . .
12	*get married* if your parents agree, at . . . .
13	*become* a street trader at . . . .
	but in Scotland at . . . .
14	*choose* your own doctor at . . . .
15	*give blood* at . . . .
16	*stand* for the local council or Parliament at . . . .
17	*buy* things on Hire Purchase at . . . .
18	*be tried* in a court at . . . .
	but in Scotland at . . . .
19	*be asked* to sit on a jury at . . . .
20	*leave home* at . . . .
	but in Scotland at . . . .
21	*leave home* if your parents agree at . . . .
22	*be sent* to prison at . . . .
23	*be sentenced* to perform community service at . . . .
24	*be sent* to Detention Centre at . . . .

Later, when you have compared your own answers with those given by the law (see page 41), discuss:

1 What are the main differences between what you thought and what the law actually says?

2 Which laws do you disagree with?

3 Which laws do you agree with?

Shopping

What do you think are the customers' rights in these cases?

1 Price Ticket Wrong

You see a packet of flour, in a super-market, marked at 40p. You take it to the check-out and the assistant tells you the price has gone up and you'll have to pay 45p.

What are your rights?
a) Can you force the shop to sell you the flour at 40p?
b) Has the shop committed a criminal offence?

2 You Slip and Fall

While shopping in the supermarket you slip on some spilt ice cream. You ladder your tights and twist your ankle.

What are your rights?

3 You Break Goods in Shop

Your little boy knocks over a display of coffee at the supermarket. The manager demands that you pay for every single jar he smashes.

What are your rights?

_____ *Now discuss the following cases:* _____

Holidays

4 Hotel Overbooked

You book a package holiday with a tour operator in a hotel by the sea, only five minutes walk from the shops. When you arrive, the hotel is full and you are put up in a self-catering apartment miles away in the country. The tour operator now says that you won't get any money back because the hotel manager overbooked and, as the booking conditions make clear, the tour operator is not responsible for the acts of its agents or sub-contractors.

What are your rights?

5 Misleading Brochure

You book your holiday in a hotel which the brochure says has a swimming pool and full waiter service.

When you get there, it doesn't, and your room is filthy, the shower doesn't work and the bed linen is ripped. Your complaints are ignored and you determine to complain when you get back home.

What are your rights?

Property left with shops

6 Damage at Dry Cleaners

You take an expensive dress to the dry cleaners. When you collect it, you notice that the collar is badly torn.

What are your rights?

7 Would it be different if . . .

. . . there had been a large notice on the wall saying that the dry cleaner's liability was restricted to £20?

8 Your Watch Stolen

You are given a watch and take it to the jewellers to have it engraved. When you go to collect it, you find the watch has been stolen in an armed raid. The shop owner says you can't claim from him for the watch, pointing to a large notice stating that 'all articles are left at the customer's own risk'.

What are your rights?

Buying from home

9 Mail Order

You pay for a set of pans from an ad in a Sunday newspaper. The ad states 'allow 28 days for delivery', but after six weeks you have still heard nothing. You contact the firm but find it has gone bankrupt.

What are your rights?

10 Would it be different if . . .

. . . after six weeks you got tired of waiting and bought another set of pans but, shortly after, the original set turned up?

11 A Persuasive Salesman

You get a leaflet through your letterbox extolling the fuel-saving virtues of double-glazing. You phone to find out the cost. The salesman comes, and never stops talking. At 11p.m. you sign a sale agreement and hand over a cheque for a deposit to get rid of him more than anything else.

Next morning, you realise you have done the wrong thing and ring the company straight away to cancel but are told that you can't.

What are your rights?

Later . . .

1   Discuss your answers with the rest of the class.
2   Compare your answers with the answers given by the law itself (see page 41).
3   Which of the law's own answers do you most disagree with?

from *Which?* magazine, May 1983

The Law Says . . . (p. 38)

The Law says you can

1 at	**18**	8 at	**16**	13 at	**17**		at	**8**
2 at	**16**	9 at	**17**		at	**18**	19 at	**18**
3 at	**18**	10 at	**16**	14 at	**16**	20 at	**18**
4 at	**16**		at	**17**	15 at	**18**		at	**16**
5 at	**14**		at	**21**	16 at	**21**	21 at	**16**
6 at	**13**	11 at	**18**	17 at	**18**	22 at	**17**
7 at	**16**	12 at	**16**	18 at	**10**	23 at	**12**
						24 at	**14**

What are your rights . . . (pp. 39-40)

1 price ticket wrong

None – you can't force the shop to sell you anything let alone at any particular price. But the shop is guilty of an offence – food can't be repriced up (unless the first price was fairly obviously a mistake). They may be guilty of another offence by demanding a price higher than the one shown on the price tag.

2 you slip and fall

The supermarket has a duty of care to make the premises safe. The spilt ice cream suggests they have failed in this, and they will probably have to compensate you for your injuries.

3 you break goods in shop

So long as you have been taking reasonable care to control your child, then you aren't liable for the damage. A supermarket should either exclude children or arrange displays so that they are safe from children behaving 'reasonably'.

4 hotel overbooked

You are entitled to the holiday you paid for and it was up to the tour operator to provide this. An exclusion clause can't be used to get out of this responsibility even if it was the hotel manager's fault (the tour operator would have to make its own claim against the hotel).

5 misleading brochure

You are entitled to the facilities claimed in the brochure – the swimming pool and waiter service – and to accommodation of a reasonable standard. The tour operator may well be committing an offence as the brochure claimed that the hotel had facilities which it didn't.

6 damage at dry cleaners

You are entitled to dry cleaning carried out with reasonable care and skill. But it is up to you to prove that it hasn't been.

7 Would it be different if . . .

If the notice was prominent then, in law, it would probably be effective. But it is in breach of the ABLC Code of Practice so you could take the matter up with them if the dry cleaner was a member.

8 your watch stolen

None. Whether or not there is a notice warning you of the fact, the jeweller is liable for your watch only if he fails to take reasonable care to look after it. And in this case, it doesn't look as though he has been negligent.

9 mail order

By not delivering the pans, the firm is in breach of contract and you are entitled to your money back.

10 Would it be different if . . .

In law, a firm doesn't have to deliver in a specified time. So you wouldn't have a legal right to your money back unless you had made 'time of the essence' and bought the goods on the condition that they arrived by a particular date.

But to comply with the British Code of Advertising Practice, a firm should make sure that you do get the goods or a card giving you the chance to cancel, within the original delivery time.

11 a persuasive salesman

You can't simply cancel – you've signed a valid and enforceable contract of sale. But if the company is a member of the Glass and Glazing Federation you have five days, from signing, to cancel, under their Code of Practice.

5 Points of View

Stories can be told from many different points of view. Very often, the point of view suddenly changes in the middle of a story, and later changes again.

Here are some examples from stories written by students.

from Ivan the Terrible *directed by Sergei Eisenstein, 1942*

THE FANTASTIC

My tale begins in a roomy, air-conditioned palace. Or was it a cathedral? The clear water of the swimming pool shimmered like the sea. The large sun lamp and the expensive wave machine added to the effect. A cooling-fan placed above the swimming pool gave the impression of a fresh sea breeze. Everything was just right for a star with a frenzied life style to cope with.

As I lay soaking up the ultraviolet rays from the sun lamp, a knocking on the glass awoke me from my gentle slumber. I looked at the source of the disturbance: a young girl stood there, looking sad and cold. I had forgotten how cold the temperature had fallen outside my palace. My first reaction was one of irritation: how had the girl avoided my guards whom I had placed around my home? But after thinking about it, I pressed a button and a panel of glass slid open silently. Now the girl eagerly rushed forward into a small room of bulletproof glass. I let the button go, and the girl was trapped in my last line of security. On my monitor, I checked her for weapons and saw she was clean. She was also amazingly beautiful for someone so young. She could only have been fourteen or so, and wore a plain white suit. Her hair was blond and styled to perfection. I opened the second door, thinking that now I was safe. The girl ran towards me, saying, 'Please don't call the guards!'

'Okay,' I said, 'but I won't talk to you for long.' I smiled at her. My smile was a main factor in my success as a musician: I had a body, a voice, a good manager, and a smile! 'You want my autograph?'

She replied, 'No. I want to talk.'

We talked for a very long time. She was not like the rest of my fans. She talked of politics, of unemployment, of life. I did not notice that night was falling.

'What does all this mean?' she asked.
'All what?' I replied.
'All this luxury.'
'It's my Utopia,' I said.
'But what does it mean to you?'
'I – I'm not sure,' I stammered.
'Do you believe in God?' she asked.
'I don't think I do,' I replied.

And now she stood up and – and vanished! She disappeared into nothingness. What had happened? Had I imagined everything? I sat for a long while, lost in thought. What sort of life was I leading? Was it all worth it? How would it end? Questions, questions. Outside the rain was falling. Inside my palace the fans whirred, while I wrestled with my thoughts. At last, my figure was lost in the darkness.

Howard Smith

For Discussion

1   From whose point of view is the story written?
2   The writer does not answer the question 'Who is the girl?' Nor does he explain fully what is happening. What are some of the possibilities?
3   What is 'Utopia'?
4   Is there any difference between the way this story ends and the way most stories end?

from The Princess *directed by Pál Erdöss, 1985*

The Temple of Inner Peace

It was raining. The main entrance to the hospital was bleak and empty. The approach to the hospital was flat and covered with grass. Right now the wind was tearing insanely across the land. Even the hardiest of souls would have preferred to stay inside the antiseptic walls of the hospital, but George was not like that. The weather gave her a certain satisfaction. The weather was so bad it seemed to reject her, to dislike her, just as she rejected herself. She had known this would happen even before she had tried to kill herself with an overdose.

As she reached the bus stop and got aboard the bus, everything around her seemed to increase her sense of rejection. The driver took her money with a look of disgust. Others on the bus looked at her as if to say, 'Don't sit near me!' Oh, she had known it would happen, all right. But that did not make it easier to bear. By the time she got off the bus to begin the walk to her flat, she was nearly in tears, her mind screaming out for pity.

She did not notice the man in the grey sports jacket who got off behind her and followed her home.

She cried herself to sleep that night and for the next three nights. During the days, she stared with empty eyes at the people in the park opposite her flat. All she wanted was a friend. But no one cared – not even the man in the grey sports jacket who carefully fed the ducks in the park. She could see him from her window. She could see him two or three times every day.

Finally, she decided she must go out. She needed people. She was feeling better.

A dog scampered over to where she sat on the park bench and began licking her hands. She burst into tears – not for sadness, but for joy. The dog's owner came over to her. 'I'm sorry,' he said. And then he must have thought she was shivering, for he said, 'Are you cold? Are you sick?' And he took off his grey sports jacket and said, 'Here, take this.'

He put the jacket around her shoulders, and sat down beside her. He introduced himself. His name was Harry Lord.

George told him, 'I'm Georgina Maine. They call me George.' They talked together. He invited her for a drink.

He was considerate and charming. He was a gentleman. They went to a bar. Later they went to his flat, and they made love: fervently, tenderly and with passion.

The following morning she awoke to find him staring at her, studying the lines of her face as she lay beside him.

'I was just thinking. I am going to the Temple of Inner Peace today, and I wonder if you might like to come along.' His voice carried a hint of persuasion and compulsion. 'Of course, you don't have to, if you're planning anything else.'

She told herself there was no danger: Harry was there to protect her.

The Temple of Inner Peace was a big house in its own grounds in the high-class area of town. It was very old. As they stepped through the door, Harry seemed to change, to relax.

'Now then, my dear, you see before you the Temple of Inner Peace.' But all that George could see was the inside of an empty house. 'I keep it specially for people like you,' he said.

He could hear the fear in her voice when she replied, 'I don't understand. I don't understand. What do you mean – people like me?'

Harry smiled for the last time and said, 'People nobody will miss!'

Philip Hancock

For Discussion

1   How does the story end?

2   What is the first clue in the story that something is going to go wrong, or that something odd will happen?

3   How important is the weather in the first part of the story?

4   From whose point of view is the story told?

45

from Ran *directed by Akira Kurosawa, 1985*

46

DARK MOODS

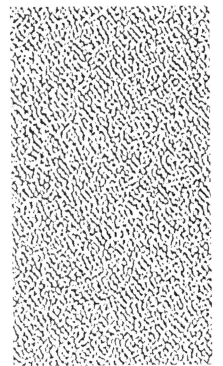

For Discussion

1 From whose point of view is this story told?
2 What is special about the viewpoint?
3 What probably is happening in the last part of the story – beginning with, 'What will you do when you grow up?'
4 What is important about the last sentence of the story? Does it make any difference to the rest of the story?

My mother had now been in hospital for four months. I prayed for her recovery although I knew deep inside that the chance for this was very slight. The pains she suffered from were acute. I knew there was very little chance of her survival.

Although I saw her every day, it was for only a short time. With every visit, I could see in her face any slight changes that occurred in her physical state.

One morning I awoke early to take a walk before it was visiting time at the hospital. I walked around the hospital and finally sat down. I stared at the window through which my mother lay. A tear trickled down my cheek, followed by another and yet another, as though I somehow knew that she . . .

'Sir!' a voice called out to me. I turned abruptly, bringing my sleeve across my eyes. It was the pale young doctor who had been nursing my mother since she had arrived here.

'Well, how is she?' I asked. For a few seconds he did not speak 'but looked into my eyes. Then he spoke.

'I am sorry, Sir, but your mother's eyes closed upon the light of this world a few hours ago.' With that he turned back to the building and left me.

It was the first time that a grave had opened in my road of life. The figure of my mother in her chair by the kitchen fire, haunted me night and day. That the place could possibly be without her, was something my mind seemed unable to compass.

There was no other in my family; for once there were seven who now are one – I. There was however my faithful companion, Ticky, my hound. He seemed to understand my feelings as I sat by the fire with my eyes closed, for he too would close his eyes, and when I was quiet, so too was he.

The absence of my mother from the home left me with little to do, for I soon quitted my job and fell into a delirious fever, during which time a brother-in-law travelled down from Australia to be at my bedside. He did not need to stay long as I did not stay long. For as my delirium worsened, I felt myself fading, fading away into the past, in the hope that I might 'catch up' with my mother. My faithful dog too stayed at my bedside day and night. He seemed to care for me as I had cared for my mother. But the days were short and soon my eyes too closed upon the light of the world, hopefully to meet my mother's . . .

'What will you do when you grow up?'
'I want to be – ' I did not like to tell her.
'Well, you can tell your mother.'
'I want to be a poet. I want to tell stories.'
Everybody else had laughed when I said this. I should have known that my mother would believe me.
'What sort of stories will you tell?'
'Strange stories,' I said, and the fire was burning, and mother sat back in her chair. Outside, the wind was howling.

Ravi Sheanh

TWO OPENERS

These are the opening sections of two stories.

1

Waiting for Mickey

As Pete walked into his small dark bedsit room, he saw the curtain move as if someone had just brushed past it. He could sense it, yet again, that feeling that someone had been in his room, looking round, touching his belongings.

He had been there two months and this was the fifth time it had happened, He was a student at the art college and he knew hardly anyone, least of all the other people in the other two rooms. He knew there was a young girl downstairs. Every day he could hear her calling her cat, William. He had never spoken to her. He had only passed her once on the stairs. He had looked longingly into her blue eyes and then she had tossed her blonde hair and run down the stairs. Pete had said to himself that he would speak to her one day. He also used to hear someone climbing the stairs to the room above his, but he did not know the person living there. He had never seen him – or her . . .

**Kirsten March
(extract)**

2

On the Edge

The time was 5 a.m. as John stood on the edge of the cliff, gazing down at the calm sea three hundred feet below. There was silence all around, but it was far from silent in John's confused mind. Why? Why? Why? The question passed repeatedly through his thoughts. He had given her everything – love, affection, kindness, his heart. And look at the way she repaid him! But now he had to face reality: she was gone from his life and there was nothing for him to live for. He had been staring down at the water for a long time. Now he made his decision. He knew what he must do.

He had been nineteen years old when he started at university. A very bright person: his future seemed bright. His mistake was to make the wrong friends. Mike and Ajay and Stephen were clever and he enjoyed their company. But they spent more time with women than they did with their studies. John had never had a girlfriend in his life and was intent on keeping it that way. His room-mate, Gary, talked only of Susan, his girlfriend. That was how it all began. If only he had never shared a room with Gary. But deep down, John knew that it was really his own fault for taking everything so seriously – like the time when Susan brought a friend of hers to meet him . . .

Shaeed Chowdhury (extract)

For Discussion

1 What is going to happen next in the two stories? How many different possibilities can you think of?

2 How will the two stories end?

3 Is there any similarity in the way the two stories begin?

PUNCTUATION: The Comma (Revision)

By way of revision, talk about where, if at all, you would use commas in these sentences:

1 'Never tell' he said 'what I have just told you.'
2 If you decide to fight John will run away.
3 You can fight run shout scream and cry but John will never run away.

The short extract from Shaeed's story (*On the Edge*) illustrates another main use of the comma. Notice how he uses commas to separate people's names from their descriptions – as in:

His room-mate, Gary, talked only of Susan, his girlfriend.

Other examples would be: He spoke to the Principal, Mrs Eleanor Browne.
The most popular dancer, George Morse, said that dancing is something everyone can do.
Maria Tallchief, a great ballet dancer, gave the prizes at the dancing competition.

Working on your own, rewrite these sentences with any commas that you think necessary.

1 The weather was really bad.

2 Nobody not even the organisers thought it would be possible to have a match.

3 Nancy Graves the chief organiser thought they would have to cancel all their plans.

4 Before we cancel we must get a weather forecast she said.

5 There was gloom disappointment anger and sorrow on everyone's faces as they waited for the news.

from Ran *directed by Akira Kurosawa, 1985*

POINTS OF VIEW IN FILM MAKING

A film maker, like any story teller, tells his or her story from a point of view. As in any story, the point of view may change many times in the course of the film. Look, for example, at the film stills in this Unit.

1 Sometimes a shot in a film not only presents a scene but also presents it through the eyes of a character. The audience seem to be looking at the scene as if they are the character. Is this true of any of the stills here?

2 Sometimes a shot seems to present a scene from a great distance, as if a god is looking at (or looking down at) what is happening. Is this true of any of the stills here?

3 Mostly, when a character is shown on film, the audience is told a vast amount of information just by the way the character is presented. We know almost at once whether the character is good or bad, weak or strong – or we think we know. For example, what do the two stills from *The Princess* and *The Ballad of a Soldier* tell you about the two young women?

from The Ballad of a Soldier *directed by Grigori Chukrai, 1959*

QUESTIONS *on all the materials in this Unit*

To answer these questions you will need to re-read all the stories in this Unit and also to look again at the pictures.

1 How does the storyteller of *The Fantastic* earn a living?

2 In *The Temple of Inner Peace*, why has George been in hospital?

3 Copy out the sentence in *Dark Moods* that first tells the reader that the mother has died.

4 Which of the stories is (or are) told by one of the characters? Write out the title (or titles).

5 Which if any of the stories include a flashback? Write out the title or titles.

6 Which if any of the stories end with a flashback? Write out the title or titles.

7 Give a list of five different things that are mentioned in the first paragraph of *The Fantastic* that show that the story-teller is very rich.

8 Give another word or phrase meaning the same as 'frenzied' (first paragraph of *The Fantastic*).

9 In the last paragraph but five of *The Temple of Inner Peace* find and copy out a word that means *command* or *ordering*.

10 In the paragraph of *Dark Moods* that starts 'It was the first time', find and copy out a word that means *grasp* or *understand*.

11 Which of the film stills show what is happening from the point of view of a character in the picture? Write out their titles.

PUNCTUATION   *Rewrite these sentences with the correct punctuation:*

12 Mary said It's time to go.

13 I'd like to stay a little longer said Anne.

14 I'm fed up said Mary and I'm going home.

15 Anne looked angry and said You're spoiling the fun.

16 It's been no fun for me said Mary.

_____ SUGGESTIONS FOR WRITING _____

Write a story of your own suggested by one of the pictures in this Unit.

Or write the rest of the story Waiting for Mickey, *or* On the Edge.

In your writing, perhaps experiment with the use of flashback as part of the story, or with an ending that is a twist or surprise, as in The Temple of Inner Peace.

6 Crime and Punishment

People often argue bitterly about what they consider to be the right punishment for a particular crime. Judges cannot give a prisoner whatever punishment they choose – their powers are closely limited by Parliament. But in many cases there is a wide difference between the minimum and the maximum punishments that they can inflict.

Group Discussion

Do You Agree with the Courts?

The main types of punishment in
- **British law today are:**

- imprisonment;

- detention centres for young offenders;

- probation;

- conditional discharge and suspended sentence – this means the offender is set free but can be sent to prison later for the same offence if he or she commits another crime;

- community service order – this means the offender is set free but has to perform some kind of work for the community.

- fines

Here is a list of cases that have come before the courts.

In groups, rearrange the list in order of seriousness. Begin with the case that you think is the most serious. Also, see if you can agree on the right punishment for each offence.

Later you will be able to compare you lists among yourselves. Also you will be able to compare your views with the ways in which the courts actually dealt with the offenders, given in the Teacher's Book.

> **Obstructing the highway (CND demonstrator)**
> **Killing four pedestrians and dangerous driving**
> **Killing one pedestrian and dangerous driving**
> **Theft of £600 (estate agent)**
> **Killing two pedestrians and dangerous driving**
> **Theft of £16,000 (solicitor)**
> **Theft of £850 (employee)**
> **Drunken father killing his four children**
> **Killing a badger**
> **Stealing goods valued at £5**

Notes

- Theft can take the form of using money for your own benefit after it has been given you to look after for someone else. An example would be an estate agent taking money as a deposit on a house that a client hopes to buy, and then spending the money on himself or herself.

- The last case (stealing goods valued at £5) involved an offender who had already spent many years in prison for petty thefts.

Later, compare your lists and suggested punishments with the rest of the class.

52

Group Discussion

Fair Comment?

After you have compared your views on the punishments for the various crimes listed above with the decisions of the courts, look at the following statements. They are all comments on the cases made by students who, like yourselves, had talked about the differences between their views and the decisions of the courts.

Which of these comments do you regard as fair? Talk about them in groups, and write down the number of the comment and your decision: FAIR or UNFAIR.

1   These cases show that the whole system of punishment is totally unjust.

2   These cases show that at certain times the system of punishments is unjust.

3   These cases show that there are times when dangerous driving is punished too leniently by the courts.

4   The courts are sometimes very hard on petty criminals who keep on committing petty crimes.

5   Judging from these ten cases, the courts are harder on people who do damage to property than they are to people who do damage to other people.

6   This list proves that you will get a worse punishment for killing a badger than you will for killing a pedestrian while driving your car.

7   This list suggests you may get a worse punishment for killing a badger than you will get for killing a pedestrian while driving your car.

8   I think that some of these offenders should have been punished more severely.

9   Many people seem to be sent to prison for small offences which they commit again and again. I do not think it is a good idea to send such people to prison.

10 Judging only from these ten cases, there seems to be a lot that is wrong about our system of punishing criminals.

Now compare your views with the rest of the class.

Appropriate Punishments

Here are some imaginary cases. Discuss each one and decide on the appropriate punishment.

1   An old man has been convicted many times of petty theft, and has spent over thirty years in prison. He steals a cake from a cake-shop.

2   The same old man breaks into a house by a back door, and steals a cake from a larder. While making his getaway an old lady living in the house walks into the kitchen, sees him, and is so frightened she has a heart attack and dies.

3   A young man, with no criminal record of any kind, loses his temper with a boy who pushes in front of him in a bus queue. He hits him so hard the boy is taken to hospital and is unable to walk again for a month. The young man is genuinely ashamed of what he did.

4   Two girls, aged 17, kidnap a baby. They do it for fun, to see if they can get away with it. They make a ransom demand and are caught by the police. The baby is unharmed.

5   The same two girls, but this time the baby dies through neglect. The girls show no regret and tell the police the whole thing is very amusing.

6   A boy has recently left school and can find no work. He goes housebreaking, and is found by an elderly man rummaging through his kitchen. The man attacks the boy with a bread knife and in the struggle, the man is seriously wounded.

7   The same boy, the same old man, but the old man eventually dies in hospital.

8   In a family row, a girl runs away from home, breaks into a friend's house and steals money.

9   The same girl, after conviction and punishment for the above offence, runs away again, stealing this time from her parents. She tells the police she will not live at home again.

Now compare your views with the rest of the class.

Group work continued

Three News Reports

1 *In this first story the five paragraphs are given in the wrong order. Working together in pairs or small groups, work out the right order.*

Just write down the numbers 1 to 5 underneath each other and then write against each number the appropriate letter. For example, if you think B is the first paragraph, you will write 1B, and so on.

A The chairman of the bench, Mr George Mitchell, said: 'This court is horrified to hear of the grisly activities that you two young men perpetrated. We have heard of the callous way in which you treated these animals. We believe you will not respond to anything other than a custodial sentence.'

B Police and RSPCA officers' who raided the youths' homes, found the trophy, a bird of prey which was still alive, and a stuffed song thrush, a buzzard, two starlings, and a squirrel which had already been mounted.

C Mark Starks, aged 19, was sent to a detention centre and Andrew Hull, 18, was sentenced to youth custody. Both live in Old Coulsdon, Surrey.

D Two teenagers were sentenced to three months' custody by Croydon magistrates yesterday after they had admitted killing a badger to add to their collection of stuffed animals.

E Both admitted stopping the badger by blinding it with a spotlight. Their three lurcher dogs attacked and killed it before they could stop them, they said. They then cut off the badger's head, intending to mount it. They claimed they had been rabbiting.

from The Guardian, 13 April 1985

2 *The second news report is given here in the correct order of paragraphs, but a set of subheadings is also given which is not in the correct order. Choose the best subheading for each paragraph.*

Just write down the numbers 1 to 5 underneath each other, and then write down the letter of the appropriate subheading. For example, if you think E is the best subheading for paragraph 1, you will write 1E, and so on.

Note *Before you work on the subheadings, read the article and discuss any questions you may have about any of the language.*

1 A Labour MP said in the Commons yesterday that drink-drivers involved in fatal accidents were "murderers and ought to be treated as such." Mr Willie Hamilton (Fife Central) demanded that courts impose heavy gaol sentences on motorists convicted of drink-driving offences.

2 "Unless there are compelling mitigating circumstances, there should be available to the courts the power to impose very heavy gaol sentences, the suspension of driving licences for life and compensation for the innocent victims."

3 He suggested the Government's Christmas campaign against drink-driving should be given the slogan: "Drunken drivers can be murderers. Keep sober or risk a gaol sentence."

4 Mr Hamilton said his call followed a case last March in which a driver with nearly three times the legal alcohol limit in his blood admitted causing the death by reckless driving of 69-year-old Mrs Ellen Emanuel of Coldstream Avenue, Leven.

5 The man, Anthony Sharp, aged 37, received a 240-hour community service order and was banned from driving for five years.

A Tougher penalties

B Woman killed

C Killer's punishment

D Drunken murderers

E Christmas campaign

from The Guardian, 23 November 1985

3 *For this third report, read the story together and talk about it.*

Justice . . . after 15 years

Ex P-c jailed for killing is ruled innocent

Standard Picture: JACK MANWARING

ELATED ... Keith Fellowes with his wife Carol after today's hearing.

A MAN who served four years for manslaughter was declared innocent today.

The former policeman had been given a seven-year jail sentence in 1970 after being convicted of killing an elderly coin dealer.

At the Court of Appeal in London today, Lord Lane, the Lord Chief Justice, said it would be an understatement to describe the case of Mr Keith Fellowes – a 22-year-old taxi driver at the time of the killing – as extremely disturbing.

Important evidence, gathered by police hunting the killer of 67-year-old Mr Harold Parkinson at his home near Morecambe, was not made available to lawyers at Mr Fellowes' trial at Lancaster.

Joy

Lord Lane said: "It is now clear that, despite that apparently strong case against him at the trial, he could not have committed the crime of which he was convicted.

"If nothing else, this case demonstrates the fallibility of any system operated by human beings."

Mr Fellowes, 37, a businessman of Binfield, Berkshire, had his conviction for Mr Parkinson's manslaughter quashed and sentence set aside.

Lord Lane said evidence called at the trial put the date of death as January 24. But new evidence put it as the 25th, when Fellowes had a "cast-iron alibi." He added: "It is quite plain Fellowes could not have been there."

He was released on parole in 1974. The case was referred to the court by Home Secretary Leon Brittan after a police informer set off a new investigation.

A fit and suntanned Mr Fellowes, who sat in court holding the hand of his wife Coral throughout today's hearing, said he was "excited and elated."

from the *London Standard*, **12 July 1985**

Read and discuss the questions that follow, and then write down your own answers individually.

QUESTIONS

1 Whom was Mr Fellowes convicted of killing?

2 When was the killing at first thought to have taken place?

3 When did the killing actually take place?

4 Why is the difference (between the answers to **2** and **3**) so important?

5 Who held back important evidence at the trial?

6 Would it be fair comment to say that this case shows it is perfectly possible to punish the wrong person? Explain your answer.

7 Would it be fair comment to say that this case is a good argument against capital punishment? Explain your answer.

8 Would it be fair comment to say that this case shows that it is a mistake to punish anyone? Explain your answer.

9 Copy out one sentence from this report that says, in other words, that we are always capable of making mistakes.

10 What is an alibi?

PUNCTUATION: Capital Letters

Capital letters are used widely in all writing, including, for instance, the two news reports you have just read. They are used:

1   to show the start of a new sentence.

2   to show the start of anything that is actually said, as in:
    The chairman said, 'The meeting must now be closed.'

3   for the word 'I'. This is always written as a capital letter, as in:
    The chairman said, 'Mary and I attended the meeting.'

4   at the beginning of proper names. These include the names of people, places, and things such as companies and organisations.

Group Work

Proper Names

Re-read the two news stories from The Guardian *and make a list of all the words in which capital letters are used to show proper names.*

Write them down under these headings: people's names
people's titles (such as Dr)
names of towns or cities
names of counties
names of institutions, companies
    or organisations
names of streets or roads

Now rewrite this short passage with capital letters used where necessary:

Mrs joan marshall was a large and lively lady and she was the president of the mayfair travellers association. She lived in a large house in berkeley square london w 1, and knew the duke of wessex, the queen of transylvania and major-general sir willard matthews. She was so rich that it was said that she owned half of yorkshire, most of scotland and all of the british-american oil drilling company limited. From the beginning of May to the end of September she retired to an island in the caribbean. i assume that she owned that as well.

The following article was written as an introduction to a programme in the BBC Horizon *series of documentaries. It is about an American, Kenneth Bianchi, who was convicted in 1980 of a series of murders of young women. He pleaded in his defence that he could not be held responsible for what he had done because he suffered from a 'split personality': one half of him did not know what the other half was doing.*

Listen to the article while it is read to you. Then discuss it. While you are listening, make a note of any words or phrases that you do not understand.

LISTENING COMPREHENSION

Two Faces of a Killer

Each age of science has produced its own monsters. The discovery of electricity shocked into life Frankenstein's creature. The heyday of chemistry turned Dr Jekyll into Mr Hyde. Palaeontology cast up living dinosaurs; rocketry and space exploration, creatures from other planets.

Today these monsters seem rather second-rate, a bit gimcrack. In our psychological age, they have been defused of their power to frighten us. They have become amusing. For what horrifies us now is the psychological monster who is capable of anything, but who looks exactly like ourselves.

The point is made by one of

the characters in *Horizon's* two films on the so-called Hillside Strangler. 'What made it so frightening,' she says, 'is that the killer could have been anybody, an average, ordinary man. He could have been the man taking tickets from you at the theatre or waiting at your table in a restaurant – someone's son, someone's loving husband. That was what was so terrifying. There was just no way to guard against it.'

In September 1977, the naked body of a young woman was found in the Highland Park area of Los Angeles. And in the five months that followed, nine other bodies were one by one found in the area, in the hills near a freeway or else dumped from a car into a nearby ravine. All were of young girls between the ages of 12 and 21. They had been raped and strangled and in some cases cruelly tortured.

There were no leads, no clues. And the police, who began to believe that the killer or killers had some knowledge of police procedures, warned the citizenry – especially girls who

fitted the pattern of the killer's victims – 'not to stop for a cop'.

Fear in America – as elsewhere – is good business, especially for newspapers and television news programmes. And Los Angeles was pushed and encouraged into public hysteria as murder followed murder, each one more violent and sadistic, it seemed, than the last.

In February 1978, however, the murders stopped – every bit as suddenly as they had started . . . There was a flagging of interest in the case . . .

There the matter might have rested if a policeman 1,500 miles away had not found and checked out a year later a California driving licence. The place was a small town in Washington State near the Canadian border, where a bizarre crime had taken place.

Two young women, who had, it seemed, been offered a job house-sitting for a local security agency had been found dead – hanged – in a car on a back road above the town. And a 27-year-old security guard called Kenneth Bianchi had been arrested.

The case against Bianchi was not strong. He was 'efficient', 'helpful', 'friendly', well-liked, the father of a small son and the sort of man who sent flowers to the women in the office at Christmas. He was studying to be an officer in the Sherriff's Reserve. And though he had no quickly provable alibi for the night of the crime in question, he was polite and co-operative and denied all involvement.

Only his California driving licence suggested there was more to Kenneth Bianchi than the smiling 'all-American boy' who met the eye. For it proved that in 1977 he had lived in Los Angeles, next door to one of the victims of the Hillside Strangler and opposite another.

The films trace the gradual processes by which Kenneth Bianchi was forced to take responsibility, first for the Washington State murders, and then for the murders in Los Angeles. This involved careful detective work, a relentless poring-over of a few meagre clues, a matching of body hairs and traces of fabric. More importantly, though, it meant an elaborate investigation of Bianchi's state of mind by psychiatrists and psychologists.

Did Kenneth Bianchi commit the murders? This was the question the police had to answer. If so, was he sane and fit for trial? Or was he insane and not responsible for his crimes? These questions were left to the experts to answer. And in the event they profoundly disagreed. For under hypnosis a violent, aggressive person called Steve had emerged from beneath the shelter of the usually benign, smiling, helpful Kenneth. Steve was snide and sneering. And he willingly confessed to a number of the murders while Kenneth continued – politely but consistently – to deny any part in them.

There were, then, two possibilities, according to the experts for the prosecution and the experts for the defence – they took opposite sides. Either Bianchi suffered from split or multiple personality and was, as Kenneth, not responsible for his own actions. Or else, again as Kenneth, he was lying, faking, malingering. And he was as sane and as responsible as the rest of us.

The point in the case of the Hillside Strangler was that he was clever and had a considerable vested interest in being diagnosed insane – it would absolve him of responsibility; it would be his way of beating the system . . .

Psychiatrists in droves, it seems, are now taking to the stands as expert witnesses, there to contradict each other at public expense about who is sane and what is madness. Where in all this is the controlling idea of personal responsibility? . . . Is it barbarous to believe that prisons are there to punish – not merely to understand, to treat, to rehabilitate?

The films cannot answer these questions. But they can and do provide us with a rare, close-up look at a psychopath – the label that was finally hung round Kenneth Bianchi's neck. As a term, psychopath is woefully inexact – a hold-all word covering all sorts of behaviour.

But as a man – and he is almost always a man – the psychopath is the true monster of our psychological age. He is the blithe killer, the manipulator beyond guilt and responsibility, the one who looks up smiling from our worst nightmares.

by Jo Durden-Smith abridged from _Radio Times_, 14 April 1984

N.B. The California court decided that Bianchi should stand trial – that he was sane and responsible for his actions. He was found guilty and sent to prison for life.

For Discussion

1 Talk about any words or phrases that you found difficult. Later, check their meanings in a dictionary. (Talk especially about the meaning of 'psychopath'.)

2 Where was Bianchi eventually arrested?

3 Where had the bulk of his crimes taken place?

4 Why did his driving licence lead to his being arrested for the Los Angeles murders?

5 Bianchi showed two different personalities when he was under hypnosis. What were they?

6 Do you feel it is possible that Bianchi suffered from split personality? Do you feel such a person should stand trial for his or her crimes?

QUESTIONS *for individual work*

1 What was the popular name given to the murderer before he was caught?

2 Where did most of the murders take place?

3 Where was the murderer caught?

4 For what offence was he first arrested?

5 What was his occupation at that time?

6 Under hypnosis he showed two personalities, each of which had a different first name. What were the names?

7 How did the two personalities answer the murder charges?

8 What was the main question that was discussed at his trial?

9 What was decided at the trial?

10 What is the meaning of:
   a) psychology?
   b) psychiatry?
   c) psychopath?

11 The first sentence of the article reads as follows:
   'Each age of science has produced its own monsters.'
Explain what this means, and give one or two examples to illustrate it.

12 The last sentence includes the following statement:
   '(The psychopath) is the . . . killer . . . beyond guilt and responsibility . . .'.
Explain what this means.

Los Angeles

59

Debating Speech

This is an extract from a student's speech on the following motion for debate:

that this House would welcome stiffer punishments for all kinds of crime.

For the Motion

I am in favour of this Motion, Madam Chairman, and I believe that what I say will be approved of by decent people everywhere. We are heartily sick of crime and criminals. We are heartily sick of the constant increase in crime. We are heartily sick of court cases where criminals are given little if any punishment for the most terrible crime. I say, enough is enough!

My opponents will say that I exaggerate, so let me give some real examples. I have here a newspaper report. It is from a national newspaper. Today's newspaper! Let me read it to you:

> *Three youths who admitted robbing a post office and hitting the postmaster on the head with an axe were today sentenced to three months' imprisonment at the Old Bailey.*

Three months in prison for robbery – and not only robbery, but robbery with violence! An innocent man is robbed and injured and the culprits get three months in prison! I'm surprised they did not also get a holiday in Spain, in case they didn't enjoy their holiday in prison!

I could give you a thousand similar examples. And what do they prove? They prove that nowadays we fall over backwards to protect – not the innocent, but the guilty! In no way can three months be considered by anyone a proper punishment for such a terrible crime.

My opponents will say that I am only giving you one example, and that I must back up my claims with reference to hard facts. I will be happy to do so. Here is another news story, from our own local newspaper. Last week, this story appeared. I quote it word for word:

> *Crime on the increase*
> *Detective Inspector Ronald Flanshaw told Foxbourne Rotary Club on Monday, "Crime is increasing in this town. Last year there were 8 per cent more crimes reported to the police than in the previous year."*
>
> *Inspector Flanshaw also said, "The police seem to be fighting a losing battle. We need more support from the public, and more support from the courts. In other words, we need stiffer punishments."*

Let me stress that this was a Detective Inspector speaking. And in effect, what was he saying? He was saying that one of the main reasons for the increase in crime is the softness of the punishments given by the courts.

For many years we have been told to feel sorry for criminals. We have been told to look not at the consequences of crime but at the causes of crime. We have been told that it is poverty that causes crime. We have been told that it is unhappy families that cause crime. We have been told that it is unemployment that causes crime. Well, Madam Chairman, I don't agree with any of these arguments. I think that one of the main causes of crime is the criminal's belief that even if he gets caught, he will only receive a light punishment.

Luther Bamidele (extract)

Group Work

1 The speaker's style

Read the speech to each other, trying to capture the style of a public speaker who is seeking to win the audience over to his or her point of view.

2 The speaker's technique

The speaker uses a number of methods or techniques in his argument to make the audience agree with him. (In the earlier Unit on *The Paranormal*, one of the writers used some of these techniques in his writing.)

Can you find examples of any of the following techniques in Luther's speech?

a) sarcasm

b) repeating words or phrases to make an effect

c) generalisations (such as, 'There is more crime today than ever before . . .')

d) pretending to speak on behalf of many other people

e) giving some facts, but not giving enough detail for the audience to know exactly what you are talking about

f) using important people's words to give weight to your own

g) jumping from a fact to a conclusion (such as, 'The man was a murderer. Murderers must be hanged.').

3 Writing for a debate

Choose a topic of your own for a debate. Working together, write a paragraph for the debate in which you use some of these techniques.

Writing and Public Speaking

Choose a topic of interest to the class as a whole, on which you can have a debate. Perhaps invite another class to debate it with you.

Choose any topic on which people feel strongly.

Working in pairs or small groups, write your speech either for or against the motion for debate.

In preparing your speech:

1 Remember that it is a speech and not an essay. When you give a speech, it should not sound as though it is being read.

   Some debaters only make notes and then speak from their notes. Others, though, write out the whole speech but then read it 'dramatically'.

2 In general, the sentences in a speech are shorter than they are in an essay. The paragraphs also are generally shorter.

3 Always work out in advance what you think the other side will probably say, and demolish their points in your own speech. (For example, 'My opponents may say ... but I would reply ...')

4 If other speakers on the other side speak before you do, make some notes on what they say, and reply to them.

5 Re-read Luther's speech before you write your own.

In staging the debate, remember:

1 The motion for debate is always some kind of statement with which one agrees or disagrees (e.g. _in the opinion of this House, capital punishment should be restored for all forms of murder_).

2 The chairperson keeps order.

3 The main speakers 'for' the motion sit on his or her right, those 'against' on the left.

4 There are usually two or three main speakers on each side of the motion. These speak first.

5 Then the debate is thrown open by the chairperson to any others who wish to speak.

6 Speakers can only be interrupted on points of _order_ (i.e. if they are not observing the rules of debate, as when they do not address the chairperson, or refer to speakers in an impolite fashion) or on points of _information_, as when a speaker is stating a matter of fact incorrectly.

7 The main speaker on each side can briefly sum up the arguments at the end, before the vote is taken.

After the debate

Choose the most effective speech and analyse it together.
To what extent did the speakers argue fairly?
What were the main methods they employed in their arguments?

7 Time and Place

The poems in this Unit in various ways explore our feelings about time, and especially about time passing. With some, there is also a strong link between a time and a place.

Some of the poems are by students; some are by poets of the last two hundred years.

Read them. Talk about them. Read them again. Look at the pictures in this Unit. Then write some poems of your own.

from The First Machete Charge *directed by Manuel Octavio Gomez, 1985*

Autobiographical Note

Beeston, the place, near Nottingham:
We lived there for three years or so.
Each Saturday at two o'clock
We queued up for the matinee,
All the kids for streets around
With snotty noses, giant caps,
Cut-down coats and heavy boots,
The natural enemies of cops
And schoolteachers. Profane and hoarse
We scrambled, yelled and fought until
The Picture Palace opened up
And we, like Hamelin children, forced
Our bony way into the hall.
That much is easy to recall;
Also the reek of chewing-gum,
Gob-stoppers and liquorice.
But of the flickering myths themselves

Not much remains. The hero was
A milky wide-brimmed hat, a shape
Astride the arched white stallion;
The villain's horse and hat were black.
Disbelief did not exist
And laundered virtue always won
With quicker gun and harder fist,
And all of us applauded it.
Yet I remember moments when
In solitude I'd find myself
Brooding on the sooty man,
The bristling villain, who could move
Imagination in a way
The well-shaved hero never could,
And even warm the nervous heart
With something oddly close to love.

Vernon Scannell

Pacific Coast

Half across the world to westward there's a harbour that I know.
Where the ships that load with lumber and the China liners go –
Where the wind blows cold at sunset off the snow-crowned peaks that gleam
Out across the Straits at twilight like the landfall of a dream.

There's a sound of foreign voices – there are wafts of strange perfume –
And a two-stringed fiddle playing somewhere in an upstairs room;
There's a rosy tide lap-lapping on an old worm-eaten quay,
And a scarlet sunset flaming down behind the China sea.

And I daresay if I went there I should find it all the same,
Still the same old sunset glory setting all the skies aflame,
Still the smell of burning forests on the quiet evening air –
Little things my heart remembers nowhere else on earth but there.

Still the harbour gulls a-calling, calling all the night and day,
And the wind across the water singing just the same old way
As it used to in the rigging of a ship I used to know
Half across the world from England, many and many a year ago.

She is gone beyond my finding – gone for ever, ship and man,
Far beyond that scarlet sunset flaming down behind Japan;
But I'll maybe find the dream there that I lost so long ago –
Half across the world to westward in a harbour that I know –
Half across the world from England, many and many a year ago.

C. Fox Smith

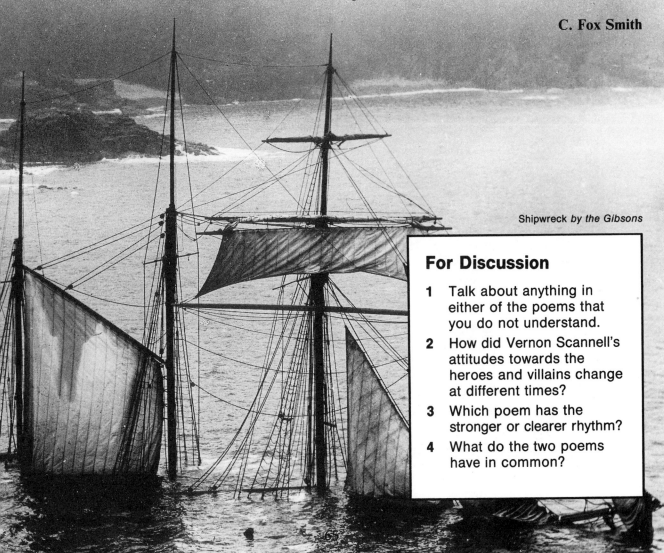

Shipwreck *by the Gibsons*

For Discussion

1 Talk about anything in either of the poems that you do not understand.

2 How did Vernon Scannell's attitudes towards the heroes and villains change at different times?

3 Which poem has the stronger or clearer rhythm?

4 What do the two poems have in common?

Valley of Desolation *by Ian Gardner*

The Lake Isle of Innisfree

I will arise and go now, and go to Innisfree,
And a small cabin build there, of clay and wattles made;
Nine bean rows will I have there, a hive for the honey bee,
And live alone in the bee-loud glade.

And I shall have some peace there, for peace comes dropping slow,
Dropping from the veils of the morning to where the cricket sings;
There midnight's all a glimmer, and noon a purple glow,
And evening full of the linnet's wings.

I will arise and go now, for always night and day
I hear lake water lapping with low sounds by the shore;
While I stand on the roadway, or on the pavements gray,
I hear it in the deep heart's core.

W. B. Yeats

The Ice Cart

Perched on my city office-stool
I watched with envy while a cool
And lucky carter handled ice . . .
And I was wandering in a trice
Far from the grey and grimy heat
Of that intolerable street
O'er sapphire berg and emerald floe,
Beneath the still cold ruby glow
Of everlasting Polar night,
Bewildered by the queer half-light,
Until I stumbled unawares
Upon a creek where big white bears
Plunged headlong down with flourished heels,
And floundered after shining seals
Through shivering seas of blinding blue.
And, as I watched them, ere I knew
I'd stripped and I was swimming too
Among the seal-pack, young and hale,
And thrusting on with threshing tail,
With twist and twirl and sudden leap
Through crackling ice and salty deep,
Diving and doubling with my kind
Until, at last, we left behind
Those big white blundering bulks of death,
And lay at length with panting breath
Upon a far untravelled floe
Beneath a gentle drift of snow
Snow drifting gently fine and white
Out of the endless Polar night,

Falling and falling evermore
Upon that far untravelled shore
Till I was buried fathoms deep
Beneath that cold white drifting sleep
Sleep drifting deep,
Deep drifting sleep . . .

The carter cracked a sudden whip:
I clutched my stool with startled grip,
Awakening to the grimy heat
Of that intolerable street.

W. W. Gibson

For Discussion

1 What line or phrase from the poem most creates a picture of the Lake Isle in the reader's mind?

2 What line or lines from 'The Ice Cart' create a picture in the reader's mind of the heat of the city?

3 Choose one or two lines from 'The Ice Cart' that create a picture to contrast with the heat.

4 What does the Lake Isle represent or symbolise to the poet?

5 What do the two poems have in common?

AFRICA

Africa my Africa
Africa of proud warriors in ancestral savannahs
Africa of whom my grandmother sings
On the banks of the distant river
I have never known you
But your blood flows in my veins
Your beautiful black blood that irrigates the fields
The blood of your sweat
The sweat of your work
The work of your slavery
The slavery of your children
Africa tell me Africa
Is this you this back that is bent
This back that breaks under the weight of humiliation
This back trembling with red scars
And saying yes to the whip under the midday sun
But a grave voice answers me
Impetuous son that tree young and strong
That tree there
In splendid loneliness amidst white and faded flowers
That is Africa your Africa
That grows again patiently obstinately
And its fruit gradually acquires
The bitter taste of liberty.

David Diop
(translated by G. Moore and U. Beier)

ALL THAT YOU HAVE GIVEN ME, AFRICA

All that you have given me, Africa
Lakes, forests, misted lagoons
All that you have given me,
Music, dances, all night stories around a fire
All that you have etched in my skin
Pigments of my ancestors
Indelible in my blood
All that you have given me Africa
Makes me walk
With a step that is like no other
Hip broken under the weight of time,
Feet large with journeys,
All that you have left to me
Even this lassitude bound to my heels,
I bear it with pride on my forehead

My health is no more to be lost
And I go forward
Praising my race which is no better
Or worse than any other.
All that you have given me Africa,
Savannahs gold in the noonday sun
Your beasts that men call wicked,
Your mines, inexplicable treasures
Obsession of a hostile world
Your suffering for lost paradises,
All that, I protect with an unforgiving hand
As far as the clear horizons
So that your heaven-given task
May be safe forever.

Anoma Kanié
(translated from French by Kathleen Weaver)

For Discussion

1   Anoma Kanié writes:
      All that you have left to me . . .
      I bear it with pride
    Is there anything in David Diop's
    poem that suggests a pride in Africa?

2   David Diop writes of:
      This back trembling with red scars
    Is there anything in Anoma Kanié's
    poem that suggests pain and
    endurance?

3   What is it that most represents or
    symbolises Africa for David Diop?

4   What most symbolises Africa for
    Anoma Kanié?

Tate Gallery *by Carel Willink*

Paper

Saturday night, and the city
is black and studded with lights
yellow, white and red
pavements throb and
the sky is lit up with a flash of neon
a symphony of drunken voices
can be heard, singing in tune with
the screech of car brakes
the smoky pubs, the discos, the sex joints
all are alive and breathing the Saturday night
air, all are shaking out their limbs,
cramped after a week of boredom
swept along by a sea of litter
towards the hungover dawn
lifted on their neon and vinyl
towards heaven, hell and the reaches beyond.

And what of the boy, the white and golden boy
who is staring, blank-faced with exhaustion
from his high window, over the city
towards the dark and silent lands beyond
his eyes glaze over
they are blue but
are as stony and cold as the white face
they are set in; they are so blue
you could see through them into
the blackness of his skull
were it not for the blank screen
kept invariably behind them

Childishly, he is crying
as he surveys his city
his ink-stained, wiry fingers,
their nails bitten down to the quick,
grasp the catch on the grimy window
and push it open
for a moment the raw-nerved, red-eyed boy
lets the cool air in
to rid himself of the stale silence

Seconds later some crumpled, grubby
sheets of paper
are thrown out on the breeze
they float gently,
rise, and are carried by
the hushed wind
out into the graveyard darkness.

Emma Payne

Evacuees arriving at Redbourne Common, Herts.
1 September 1939

Midnight

From where I sit, I see the stars,
    And down the chilly floor
The moon between the frozen bars
    Is glimmering dim and hoar.

Without in many a peakèd mound
    The glinting snowdrifts lie;
There is no voice or living sound;
    The embers slowly die.

Yet some wild thing is in mine ear;
    I hold my breath and hark;
Out of the depth I seem to hear
    A crying in the dark:

No sound of man or wife or child,
    No sound of beast that groans,
Or of the wind that whistles wild,
    Or of the tree that moans:

I know not what it is I hear;
    I bend my head and hark:
I cannot drive it from mine ear,
    That crying in the dark.

Archibald Lampman

For Discussion

1. Both poems tell stories or the outline of stories. What stories are they?
2. What does Emma Payne use as a contrast to underline the sadness and loneliness of the boy?
3. What is the chief mood or feeling in 'Midnight'?
4. What contrast is there in 'Midnight' with the 'crying in the dark'?

WHEN YOU ARE OLD

When you are old and grey and full of sleep,
And nodding by the fire, take down this book,
And slowly read, and dream of the soft look
Your eyes had once, and of their shadows deep;

How many loved your moments of glad grace,
And loved your beauty with love false or true,
But one man loved the pilgrim soul in you,
And loved the sorrows of your changing face;

And bending down beside the glowing bars,
Murmur, a little sadly, how Love fled
And paced upon the mountains overhead
And hid his face amid a crowd of stars.

W. B. Yeats

TELL ME AGAIN

Am I your only love – in the whole world – now?
Am I really the only object of your love?
If passions rage in your mind,
If love springs eternal in your heart –
Is it all meant for me? Tell me again.

Tell me right now, am I the one who inspires
All your dark thoughts, all your sadness?
Share with me what you feel, what you think.
Come, my love, pour into my heart
Whatever gives you so much pain.
Tell me again.

Nigâr Hanim
(translated from Turkish by Tâlat S. Halman)

For Discussion

1. What is the mood of the first poem?
2. What is the mood of the second poem?
3. What do both poems have in common?
4. What is different about the two poems?

Both of the last two poems in this Unit are in some ways more difficult than the others. Read them and talk about them, and talk especially about anything that is difficult about them. Then read them again.

Kubla Khan

In Xanadu did Kubla Khan
   A stately pleasure-dome decree:
Where Alph, the sacred river, ran
Through caverns measureless to man
   Down to a sunless sea.

So twice five miles of fertile ground
With walls and towers were girdled round:
And here were gardens bright with sinuous rills,
Where blossomed many an incense-bearing tree,
And here were forests ancient as the hills,
Enfolding sunny spots of greenery.

But oh! that deep romantic chasm which slanted
Down the green hill athwart a cedarn cover!
A savage place; as holy and enchanted
As e'er beneath a waning moon was haunted
By woman wailing for her demon-lover!
And from this chasm, with ceaseless turmoil seething,
As if this earth in fast thick pants were breathing,
A mighty fountain momently was forced,
Amid whose swift half-intermitted burst
Huge fragments vaulted like rebounding hail,
Or chaffy grain beneath the thresher's flail:
And 'mid these dancing rocks at once and ever
It flung up momently the sacred river.
Five miles meandering with a mazy motion
Through wood and dale the sacred river ran,
Then reached the caverns measureless to man,
And sank in tumult to a lifeless ocean:
And 'mid this tumult Kubla heard from far
Ancestral voices prophesying war!

   The shadow of the dome of pleasure
   Floated midway on the waves;
   Where was heard the mingled measure
   From the fountain and the caves.
   It was a miracle of rare device,
   A sunny pleasure-dome with caves of ice!

Samuel Taylor Coleridge (extract)

from A Passage to India *directed by David Lean, 1984*

Ode to Autumn

Season of mists and mellow fruitfulness,
   Close bosom-friend of the maturing sun;
Conspiring with him how to load and bless
   With fruit the vines that round the thatch-eaves run;
To bend with apples the moss'd cottage-trees,
   And fill all fruit with ripeness to the core;
     To swell the gourd, and plump the hazel shells
   With a sweet kernel; to set budding more,
And still more, later flowers for the bees,
Until they think warm days will never cease,
   For Summer has o'er-brimm'd their clammy cells.

On the Road to Sommand, Haute-Savoie, *by Jean Mohr*

Who hath not seen thee oft amid thy store?
   Sometimes whoever seeks abroad may find
Thee sitting careless on a granary floor,
   Thy hair soft-lifted by the winnowing wind;
Or on a half-reap'd furrow sound asleep,
   Drows'd with the fume of poppies, while thy hook
     Spares the next swath and all its twined flowers;
And sometimes like a gleaner thou dost keep
   Steady thy laden head across a brook;
   Or by a cyder-press, with patient look,
     Thou watchest the last oozings hours by hours.

Where are the songs of Spring? Ay, where are they?
   Think not of them, thou hast thy music too, –
While barred clouds bloom the soft-dying day,
   And touch the stubble-plains with rosy hue;
Then in a wailful choir the small gnats mourn
   Among the river sallows, borne aloft
     Or sinking as the light wind lives or dies;
And full-grown lambs loud bleat from hilly bourn;
   Hedge-crickets sing; and now with treble soft
   The red-breast whistles from a garden-croft;
     And gathering swallows twitter in the skies.

John Keats

For Discussion

1 Sometimes words on their own can create a picture in the mind. Their very sound sets the imagination working. Are there any words like this in the first poem?

2 Choose any one or two lines from the first poem that most vividly create a picture or image in the reader's mind.

3 Choose two or three phrases in the second poem that suggest the tastes of autumn.

4 Choose two or three phrases that suggest the sounds of autumn.

HOW SIR TRISTRAM
DRANK OF THE
LOVE DRINK

Aubrey Beardsley

GROUP DISCUSSION

1 **Symbolism, Rhythm, Mood, Image**
   All these terms have been used in the discussion of the poems in this Unit.
   Talk about them again, and see if you can agree on a definition of each.

2 Choose the two poems you think are the greatest contrast to each other. Read them to one another.

3 Look at the various pictures in this Unit.
   Choose the two that you find the most interesting, and make a list of words and phrases that capture the moods of the pictures.
   Later, compare your work on Questions 1 and 3 with the rest of the class.

WRITING

Choose a theme of your own and write a poem about it. Perhaps choose a picture from this Unit and write a poem suggested by the picture. Or draw a picture of your own.

Later, write another poem on a different theme.

8 Fraud

Here is a story told in a set of documents.

Working together in small groups, read them through, talk about them, and decide what you think has happened.

Discuss one document at a time before you move on to the next one.

Document 1

Minutes of a meeting of the Goodwill Society at the Chairman's home on Friday September 29th at 7 p.m., Winston Henville in the chair.

Also present were Stephen Wain (Treasurer), Anita Bonville (Secretary) and Viola Johnson (committee).

Apologies for absence were received from Pratish Sharda (committee) and Dorothy Hurd (committee).

The minutes of the previous meeting were read, and it was unanimously agreed that they were a true and faithful record of what had been said.

The Chairman told the meeting that he was pleased to say that the Goodwill Society had now been in existence for two years. He asked the Treasurer to say how much money the Society had now collected.

The Treasurer said that we had now collected £1000.

Viola Johnson said we should start talking about how we would spend the money. She said our aim is to give the money to old people in need, and we should now find out who needs it.

The Secretary said we had done well to collect so much money. She said that most of it had come from raffles and jumble sales.

The Treasurer said we should find ways of making more money before we give away any of it. He said we should think of investing the money.

The Chairman said we should discuss this at a later meeting when all the committee are present.

Viola Johnson said she had made a list of things to do in the next six months to help us make more money. Several ideas were discussed. It was agreed that we would plan to have a disco in St George's Hall just before Christmas.

The Treasurer said he would organise this.

The Secretary asked if the Treasurer had opened a special bank account to keep the Society's money. The Treasurer said he had not done so yet, but he would do so as soon as possible. He said that at the moment the money is in his own personal bank account.

The Secretary said that now that the Society has so much money, the Treasurer should definitely open a separate account to look after it. **The Treasurer** said he would.

There being no further business to discuss, the meeting was closed at 7.50 p.m.

Anita Bonville Honorary Secretary

Document 2 Detective Constable Keeler's notebook

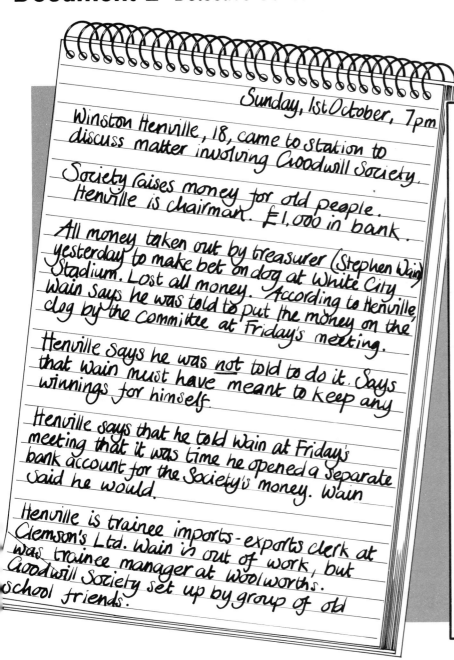

Sunday, 1st October, 7pm

Winston Henville, 18, came to station to discuss matter involving Goodwill Society.

Society raises money for old people. Henville is chairman. £1,000 in bank.

All money taken out by treasurer (Stephen Wain) yesterday to make bet on dog at White City Stadium. Lost all money. According to Henville, Wain says he was told to put the money on the dog by the committee at Friday's meeting.

Henville says he was <u>not</u> told to do it. Says that Wain must have meant to keep any winnings for himself.

Henville says that he told Wain at Friday's meeting that it was time he opened a separate bank account for the Society's money. Wain said he would.

Henville is trainee imports-exports clerk at Clemson's Ltd. Wain is out of work, but was trainee manager at Woolworths. Goodwill Society set up by group of old school friends.

Document 3

Winston Henville Esq.
Chairman, The Goodwill Society
Stapley

Dear Winston

I am writing to give you my resignation from the Society. I am shocked to hear that you have reported me to the Police and that you have denied everything that happened at Friday's meeting. I cannot understand why you have done this.

As you are well aware it was Viola Johnson who said at the meeting that we should talk about how to spend the money we have collected. I then said that we should find ways of making more money out of what we had. Then I suggested we put all the money on a dog that was running in a race at White City on Saturday. I named the dog (Clune Girlie) and the race (the 8.30). I said that a good friend of mine had told me the dog was sure to win. I also said — and this is true — that my friend is never wrong. But sadly, he was wrong on this occasion.

Also you know that we have talked before about gambling to make money, and you have always said it is a good idea. I can only think that the reason why you have now changed your story is because you are angry we have lost the money. But every gambler stands a risk of losing!

Since you have decided to make trouble for me I am resigning from the Society. I have worked hard to make money for the Society, and I believe that young people must do everything possible to help old people who are in need.

I have not yet talked to any other members of the Society but I know that they will stand by me and tell the truth. Viola and Anita will, I know, be willing to swear that we agreed on the bet on Friday evening. And I know too that although Pratish and Dorothy could not come to the meeting they will support me in other ways. They will both remember times when we have talked about making money by gambling. Also, they will both remember that you said you liked the idea and asked me to find out more about it.

I can only say 'Thank God' that there are still some good and honest friends in this world.

Yours sincerely,
Stephen Wain.

78

Document 4 Textbook on criminal law (extract)

Theft is a criminal offence which usually involves taking away something to which you have no right whatsoever. However, it can also be committed by any one who looks after money (or any other property) for someone else and who then uses that money for himself or herself. The maximum punishment for theft is ten years imprisonment.

An example would be:

Brown pays £1000 to an estate agent as a deposit on a house that he wants to buy. The house belongs to a client of the estate agent's. The estate agent spends the money on himself. This would be theft and the agent should be prosecuted.

Another example would be:

Mrs Smith is the mother of Eileen Roberts and the grandmother of Eileen's daughter Kate. She gives Eileen £5000 to look after for Kate until Kate is old enough to make her own use of the money. Eileen uses the money for herself.

Another example would be:

A schoolteacher collects money from pupils for an overseas holiday which she is organising. She spends the money on herself.

from *Introducing the Criminal Law* by E. B. Carter and M. F. Fisher

Document 5 Anita Bonville's statement to the police (extract)

I wrote the minutes of the meeting held on Friday 29th September as soon as I got home from the meeting. The minutes are an accurate record of everything that was said. There has never been any talk at any meeting about gambling or putting money on a race. I was amazed when I heard that Stephen Wain had spent and lost the money. I agree with everything that Winston Henville has told the police.

Also, I have written the minutes for every meeting of the Society and there is no talk of gambling in any of the minutes of any of the meetings.

I believe that Stephen Wain placed the money on a dog in a race and intended to keep the winnings to himself, put back the £1000 in the bank, and tell us nothing about it.

Document 6 Viola Johnson's statement to the police (extract)

There was no discussion of gambling at any meeting of the Society. I can, though, remember that Stephen Wain talked about using the Society's money on a dog race, but he did this after a meeting at the end of August. He talked about it in a cafe where we went for a drink. I cannot remember exactly who was there, but I know that Winston Henville was not there. I told him that gambling was a silly idea and there was no more talk about it.

After the meeting on Friday 29th September, Stephen walked home with me. (We live near each other.) He told me that he had lost a lot of money gambling and that he was going to borrow some money to put on a dog race that weekend. He asked me if I would like to bet some of my own money. He said the dog was sure to win. I said it was a silly idea and I thought no more about it.

For Discussion

1 What does either of these statements tell the police that they would not have known already?

2 How many people were present at the meeting on Friday 29th September?

3 How many of those who were present agree with Stephen Wain's story?

4 How many of those who were present disagree with Stephen's story?

5 Do you think Stephen should be prosecuted for the theft of the Society's money?

Document 7

Court reports at the trial of Stephen Wain on a charge of theft (extracts)

In this extract, the committee member Pratish Sharda *is giving evidence for Stephen Wain's defence. He is talking to the defence lawyer.*

Defence	Why were you not at the meeting on Friday 29th September?
Sharda	I was not well. I had a very bad headache.
Defence	Did you have any idea that Stephen Wain was going to place a bet on a dog race and that he was going to do this for the Society?
Sharda	Yes. Soon after the meeting on the 29th, I had a phone call from Winston Henville.
Defence	What time was that?
Sharda	About 9 p.m.
Defence	What did Winston Henville talk about?
Sharda	He told me that at the meeting they had talked about a dog race. He said they had agreed that Stephen should put all the money on a dog called Clune Girlie.
Defence	What did you say to that?
Sharda	I said it seemed a dangerous idea. I asked him what we would do if the dog lost the race. He said somebody had told Stephen that this dog never loses a race.
Defence	What did you say to that?
Sharda	I said I was worried.
Defence	Did you try to stop them putting the money on the race?
Sharda	No, because Winston said that they had all agreed on it at the meeting.
Defence	Why do you think Anita Bonville did not refer to the dog race and the bet when she wrote the minutes of the meeting?
Sharda	I think she wrote the minutes after the dog race and after the money had been lost.
Defence	But she says she wrote the minutes on Friday evening.
Sharda	I don't believe her.
Defence	Why do you think that Winston Henville, Anita Bonville and Viola Johnson all say that they knew nothing about the plan to put the money on a dog race?
Sharda	I think they were angry when the money was lost. I think they decided to have their revenge on Stephen Wain.

Later in the trial, one of the other committee members, Dorothy Hurd, *also spoke in Stephen's defence:*

Defence	Why were you not at the meeting on 29th September?
Hurd	My mother was ill and I had to stay home to look after her.
Defence	As far as you know, had there ever been any talk at any meeting, of putting money on a dog race?
Hurd	Yes. Stephen had talked about it quite a number of times.
Defence	At meetings?
Hurd	Yes. And he also spoke a lot about it after a meeting in August. We went to a cafe for a drink and Stephen talked about gambling.
Defence	What did he say?
Hurd	He said that a friend of his knew all about gambling, and that we could make a lot of money for the Society.
Defence	Who was in the cafe at that time?
Hurd	All of us.
Defence	Including the chairman, Winston Henville?
Hurd	Yes.
Defence	When did you first know about putting the money on this dog on September 30th? Did you know about it before it happened?
Hurd	Yes. Winston Henville phoned me up and told me that they had decided to make the bet.
Defence	Did he say how much money they had decided to bet?
Hurd	Yes. He said they'd decided to bet all the Society's money.
Defence	How much was that?
Hurd	£1000.
Defence	What did you say when he told you?
Hurd	I said it was a good idea.
Defence	When did he tell you?
Hurd	About 9 p.m. – just after the meeting that Friday.
Defence	Did he say anything else?
Hurd	Yes. He said that even if the dog didn't win the race and lost all the money, it didn't matter.
Defence	Did he say why it didn't matter?
Hurd	Yes. He said that he would pretend he knows nothing about the whole business and that he would use it to get Stephen into trouble.
Defence	What did you say to that?
Hurd	I said I was shocked. I also said I would phone up Stephen and tell him, warn him.
Defence	What did Henville say to that?
Hurd	He said he was only joking. He laughed. He said he was just being funny.
Defence	Did you believe him?
Hurd	Yes. We were all such good friends.
Defence	Did you phone up Stephen Wain and tell him?
Hurd	No.

For Discussion

1 If you add Dorothy Hurd's story to Pratish Sharda's story, what happened after the meeting on Friday 29th September?

2 According to Viola Johnson, what happened after that meeting?

3 Look again at Stephen Wain's letter of resignation. How much of what he writes in the letter is later confirmed by other members of the committee?

4 So far, what do you think has really happened? Has Stephen stolen the money?

GOODWILL SOCIETY ENDS IN CRIMINAL PROSECUTION

Treasurer Acquitted on Criminal Charge

Stephen Wain, 19, was found not guilty at the Assize Court yesterday on a charge of theft. He had been accused of gambling for his own purposes with money belonging to the Goodwill Society, of which he was the Treasurer.

The jury took three hours to reach their verdict. Wain told the court that at a meeting of the Society on the evening of Friday 29th September, the committee had decided to put all their money (£1000) on a dog racing at White City the following day. But three other members of the committee (including the chairman, Mr Winston Henville, 18) denied this.

Henville told the court that there had never been any talk of gambling with the money. He accused Wain of gambling with the money without the committee's knowledge. He said that if Wain had won with the bet, he would have kept the winnings for himself.

Different story

Speaking in Wain's defence another committee member, Dorothy Hurd, 20, told the court that she had not been at the meeting on 29th September. She said that Henville phoned her after the meeting and told her all about the plan to place the money on a bet on a dog race. She said, "I cannot understand why he is now telling a different story."

Headache

Another committee member, Pratish Sharda, 20, said that Henville had also phoned him after the meeting and told him about the plan to use the money for a bet. Sharda had not been able to attend the meeting because he had a bad headache.

After the trial Stephen Wain told our reporter that he was sad that the Goodwill Society had come to an end. "We were such good friends when we set up the Society, but everything seems to have gone wrong," he said.

For Discussion

Do you agree with the jury's verdict?

You should assume, for purposes of discussion, that the evidence in these various documents is the same as the evidence heard in court.

QUESTIONS *on the documents*

For individual writing

1 What is the difference between Anita Bonville's account of what happened at the meeting on 29th September, and Stephen Wain's?

2 According to Documents 1 and 2, who asked Stephen to open a separate bank account?

3 According to Documents 1 and 3, how far do Stephen and Anita agree about what Stephen said at the meeting on the 29th of September?

4 Copy out one sentence from Winston Henville's statement to the police that strongly implies that Stephen has committed theft.

5 The jury found Stephen not guilty. So they could not have believed Anita's statement (Document 5). Copy out the first sentence from her statement that, if Stephen is not guilty, must be a lie.

6 Copy out the first sentence in Viola Johnson's statement (Document 6) that, if Stephen is not guilty, must be a lie.

7 What important piece of evidence is given by Pratish Sharda and also Dorothy Hurd (Document 7) that is helpful to Stephen Wain?

8 Who gets most of the blame in Dorothy's story of what happened (Document 7)? Copy out ONE sentence that most clearly shows who she thinks is to blame.

Statements about the documents

Which if any of these statements do you think are fair? Explain briefly why you think so, referring to evidence from the documents.

9 There was no mention of any gambling in the minutes of the last meeting (in September).

10 There was no mention of any gambling in the minutes of any of the meetings.

11 If Stephen Wain is innocent, then Winston Henville, Anita Bonville and Viola Johnson must have got together to work out what they would tell the police.

12 If Stephen is guilty, then he must have got together with Pratish Sharda and Dorothy Hurd to work out what they would say.

WRITING A REPORT

Write a report on the case, referring to the various documents.

Discuss how you will organise the report. For example, you could:

1 Explain the basic facts, such as how the Committee was formed and what it did.

2 Explain how the police became involved.

3 Explain the evidence against Stephen Wain.

4 Explain the evidence for him.

5 Give the jury's decision.

6 Give and justify your own opinion of what probably happened.

9 Friends and Enemies

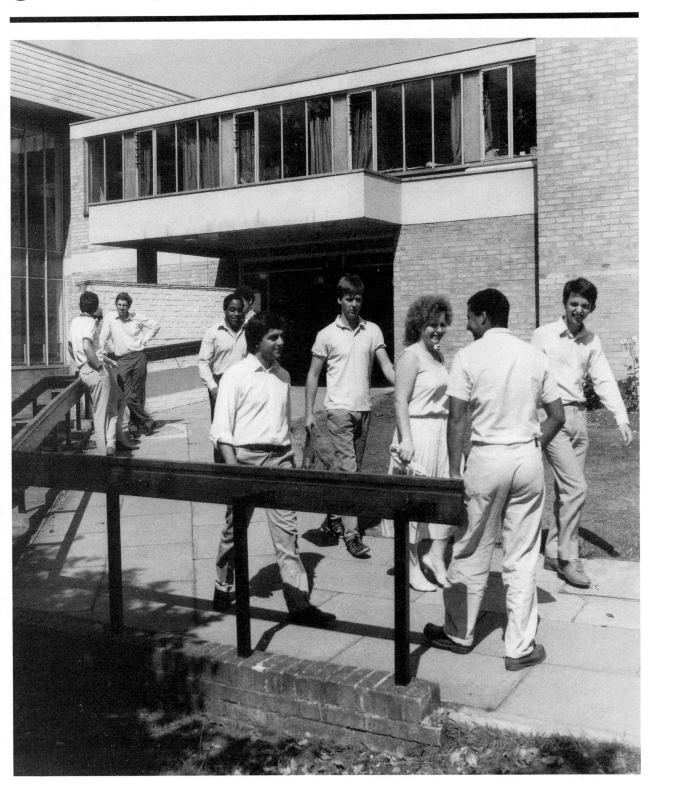

In this autobiographical story, a French writer, André Chamson, looks back on an episode from his adolescence.

MY ENEMY

As I came down to the river I saw there was a boy swimming about in the pool. He was naked save for the handkerchief tied round his waist. Above his hidden face the close-cropped hair dripped with water. He was swimming towards me and as he reached the edge, he raised himself up against the bank. It was Maubert. He saw me in the very instant that I realised who he was.

Taking a deeper breath, he put up his hands to get a hold on the rock.

While he was trying to pull himself up on the bank, I was gathering stones. With my arm flung back, I shouted at him, "Stop where you are!"

With one quick look he worked out his chances. Naked, half in the water, badly balanced, he was in no position to defend himself. Wherever he looked, there seemed no way out. I swung my arm above his head. He knew well my aim would be sure. So he let himself drop into deep water again, and gazed at me while floating on his back.

It was Maubert, my enemy. I trembled with rage and joy as I looked at him. My blood, beating violently in my veins, thudded through the hand clenched round my missile, as I thought. 'Got him!'

There came to my mind that night when he had pounced on me with a couple of his chums. They were pushing a wheelbarrow along. The street had been dark and it was near the bridge. All I had heard was my name and the thud of the wheelbarrow's two legs suddenly hitting the ground. And then I had been blinded with blows. Nevertheless, by wildly kicking out, striking round me and biting whatever met my teeth, I made them give way long enough to enable me to retreat still facing them, like an angry cat pursued by dogs. But it was not the others that mattered. It was Maubert on whom all my hatred fell. When our two schools fought together on Saturdays, for instance, under the chestnut trees of the fair ground, it was always Maubert I aimed at. We would load stones with insults and spit on them at the very moment they were hurled, so as to bewitch them and make them truly strike their goal. And Maubert, too, always aimed at me whenever we had these clashes. Now I had him in my power, one against one, with every advantage on my side.

I sat myself down on the bank. He was just opposite me, but if he so much as let the current begin to carry him away, threateningly I raised my arm. Then paddling a little with his hands,

86

unable to take his eyes off my stone, he would return to the old place.

With every moment my rage increased. He was the worst enemy I had. We did not go to the same school. Our parents did not want us to know each other. Mine said, 'They're people you couldn't trust an inch.'

I'd got him. He was a good swimmer, but he was already beginning to show signs of being tired. At moments his whole head would go under and come up again, spluttering out the water he had swallowed. I looked at him with fury. I had never seen him so close. In fact, I had hardly known what he looked like. He was fourteen, like me. You could not have called him good-looking, with his cropped hair clotted to right and left like wheat-ears after a storm. Whenever he spat the motion made by his lips sent a wave of disgust through all my body.

I watched him carefully, my stone ready. Suppose, instead, he had caught me in the pool. I'd have had that stone hurled at me long ago. I could read his thoughts in his shifty eyes. If only he could! But just let him try and drift away on the current. If I do aim I'll go for his head. So much the worse for him. And if I kill him? Oh stones don't kill. He'll manage to get out of the water all right with his head broken open and his face all bloody. They gave me a pretty good beating, they did, that night when they had the wheelbarrow, and I was one against three.

'Stop where you are, I tell you . . . You just dare to let the current carry you away . . .'

Maubert was waiting for me to strike, keeping himself afloat with slight movements of the forearms. He had the appearance of being knocked senseless already, struck in the temple by my stone, as he lay there on his back. For a moment I looked at him thus, picturing him dead, and suddenly I let the stones fall out of my left hand. Then, from the other, I hurled the stone high over his head, on to the other bank of the mountain torrent, and said, 'Get out of the water . . . Come here.'

I had hardly finished speaking before he was clinging to the bank, shuddering with cold and making a brrr . . . sound with his lips. He dragged himself up the rocky wall, and ran to the foot of a bush where he had left his clothes. I remained looking at the pool while he dressed. After some moments I looked back over my shoulder, and saw him coming towards me slowly, fastening his belt. He seemed to be thinking. I began looking at the water again, with the thought in my mind, 'Now he's going to throw a stone at my head. He's where the stones are, he has lots more round him than I have.'

When I decided to look round I saw he was now very close. He had turned up his collar, and his cheeks were beginning to glow again as though whipped by the mountain wind. Whereupon I said, 'You're not cold?'

'I've my flannel shirt, luckily.'

He had sat down near me. I stretched out on the rock, and turned towards him.

'What made you come here? Who gave you permission to come to this pool?'

'Who gave me permission? I come here often. It's my special pool.'

'Yours?'

I drew in. I thought, 'His special pool? We'll soon see!' Then suddenly I said:
'Your special pool? I've been coming here for a year now.'

His teeth clenched as he looked at me. But we were equally matched.

What kept me from leaping at his throat kept him also. We were not afraid of each other, it was a mutual respect. He continued:
'I discovered it by myself too, last year. I come here often. You're alone, and when you're in you can always see the bottom through the water.'

'There's nothing you can dive off. Otherwise it would be the best pool around here. I've often tried to do it from the other side, but that rock's in the way. You'd split your head open if you hit it.'

Maubert smiled.

'No, there's not room . . . That doesn't matter though, it's a good pool. The water's good. You can feel the air it's caught up in the waterfalls.'

So the difference between one pool and another mattered to Maubert! He could tell when the water was light or heavy. He loved them then? I could discuss all the secrets of our rivers with him?

Suddenly Maubert asked:
'Why didn't you throw it?'
'You were by yourself.'
'You think I'm afraid of you?'
'What about me then? Why, I'll take on three of you, and with a barrow thrown in.'

He flushed slightly. I had not budged, though I was ready to leap up. Even stretched out I could leap to my feet with one bound. I was thinking, 'If he moves, I'll hurl myself at his face.' He did not move however.

'Why do you hate me?' he said at last.

'It's you . . .' My hatred would not let me go on. But immediately I said, 'It's you who's worst . . . Who ever did anything . . .?'

He answered simply: Your lot . . .'
'Our lot . . .?'
'You're not the same as we are.'

Again disgust overcame me. I hated Maubert, his thick lips, cropped hair and flannel shirt. And now he was afraid. I could see that perfectly well. He raised himself a little on his elbows. He knew I was the stronger.

'I didn't shoot to teach you a lesson. If I wanted to I could smash you altogether, see! But I prefer just to talk. That way you'll realize who you have to deal with. We're not the same as you are . . . Fortunately! Our sort are not shifty brutes like you, or liars either. In our school we learn more than you do. I can ask you questions that prove it. Take French history, for example. Tell me who ruled these parts after the Romans and before the Franks? Oh, yes rack your brains all right, but that won't help you much.'

Maubert did not know. He felt like crying, but suddenly he said:

'Well how many times does 25 go into 375? In your head, in your head, don't try to work it out on your fingers! You just don't know, that's all.'

For the life of me I could not find the answer. The figures danced in front of my eyes. Mental arithmetic was not my strong point.

Maubert had got up. I did not move. I was sure he had no idea of attacking me for he was gazing at the mountain.

'There would be time to get to the top.' he said at last. 'What do you say about our going up together? I don't mean going round, but up over the rocks. I shouldn't think anyone had ever got that way up. Does it frighten you? You wouldn't dare climb that wall.'

But I was already on my feet.

'You're the one who'd never follow up there. It's steeper than it looks. Enough to make a goat turn giddy. You've got to climb over that patch of grass, get by that rock face there and then that gully, and turn left and follow that ledge.'

At last we had found a way to fight each other. I was already scrambling over the stones and gravel fallen from the mountain side, followed by Maubert tucking his trousers up and tightening his belt. I was thinking, 'He'll soon be asking me for help.'

The climb was long and very dangerous. We often had to help each other or we would both have fallen to our deaths. By the time I reached the top my hands were bleeding and several of my finger nails were broken.

Meanwhile Maubert was climbing also. His eyes had followed each of my gestures. He repeated them with the whole of his taut body. I felt he would rather have rolled down into the torrent than retrace his steps. Flat on my belly, looking down at him, I watched him coming up, terrified he might roll into the void. My own muscles twitched and contracted to help him on. 'Go on Maubert, you're all right now . . .'

Then he was at my side, pale as a ghost, with everything whirling round him.

It was then I said: 'I've won, I've won.'

We moved away from the precipice a little. It rejoiced me to have conquered the mountain wall. I had done it because Maubert was my enemy, and I would have preferred death rather than say to him as to one of my chums: 'It's crazy. It can't be done.'

Maubert, too, would never have done it without me.

But anyhow we were friends now. Friends, because deep in us we shared the same loves, the same joy – pitting ourselves against the things of our own countryside. We both talked the local speech, we had both roamed the same

mountains, and climbed the same peaks. Lying stretched out among the last thin chestnut trees where the holly and pines thinned out, relaxing after our efforts and proud of having together conquered the same rock face, we began talking.

'Next best to the mountains, I'm happiest among our vines.'

'Where? At Elze?'

'They're the only ones we have. We've an old chap working, helps us make our wine. A wonderfully handy chap, full of stories . . . It's a jolly good place, Elze . . . It only catches the sun in the morning though. Still, it's just as good.'

'We've got the sun all day, we have.'

'At Goulsou?'

'D'you know our vines then? But you've never been there, have you?'

'You've got a magnolia and a cypress in front of the house . . . And fig trees against the top wall.'

'You've been there then?'

'I've seen it from the turn in the new road . . . I even climbed the wall once, just under the plum tree . . . I know the sort of spot you like.'

So we went on talking about things and people. What could turn us into enemies now? We had no longer any secrets from each other. Everything we loved we could now possess in common. No longer was there any need to keep each to his own side of the mountain.

Meanwhile by the open passes to the north, evening began to fall. It was time to think of getting back. We rushed downwards to the town. Already we had passed two children returning to their farm in the valley, who turned to gaze in astonishment at seeing us together. It embarrassed us to be walking together, and as we had slowed down to a walk to catch our breaths again, Maubert said, though without looking at me, 'You'd better leave me before we get to Rochebelle.'

'So you're ashamed to be seen with me? I'll tell everybody we aren't together, if you like.'

'I'm not with you!' said Maubert with an obstinate expression.

He began to run again, and when he had got about a hundred yards ahead dropped to a walk, looking about on every side, like someone out walking by himself. I began gathering stones and started running to get somewhat nearer to him.

'Oh, you want to go in front, do you? See if this will help you then . . .'

Maubert fled, but even while he did so, flung a couple of stones at me that whistled round my head. I met them by jumping right and left and then stopped to hurl them in my turn. Bent double in the act, and before even the stone had touched the ground, I shouted at him like a threat, in which perhaps, too, was something of regret:

'I'll get you yet . . . I'll get you yet some day.'

from *My Enemy* by André Chamson
translated by John Rodker (adapted and abridged)

For Discussion

1 What had Maubert done to the story-teller (before the events of this story) to cause such hatred?

2 What seems to be the real cause of their hatred?

3 What is the first thing that André does that shows he is willing to be fair and reasonable to Maubert?

4 What is the first thing that Maubert does that shows that he too is willing to be fair to André?

5 Why do they end up as enemies again?

In this second autobiographical story, an English writer, Sarah Green, remembers her adolescence.

Leicester in the 1940s

MY FRIEND

Friendship is a very difficult thing. It is hard to handle. It creates many different problems. In fact I would go so far as to say that friendship is as hard to handle as love is, or even marriage. Of course I am not talking about casual friendship or easy-come-easy-go friendship. I'm talking about friends who care deeply about each other, who support each other, who make life worth living. I'm talking about friends with whom you can share almost everything.

My friendship with Kathy was a real friendship. She made me laugh. She made me feel wanted. She understood me. We could do anything together. There was hardly ever a time when she was too busy to see me. If I wanted her, even if it was just for a walk, she was almost always there. We were sixteen when we met at the local technical college and we were both doing the same course. I was very nervous the day I started and Kathy was the first person I talked to. As a result, I enjoyed my year at the Tech like nothing

I had ever thought possible. Like I say, she was fun, she was lively, she was sure of herself. And a little bit of her character rubbed off on me.

It was not a perfect friendship. That is the next thing I must say about it. Perhaps there is no such thing as a perfect friendship except in books. I find it difficult to say exactly what was wrong with it. There were two things that I have to tell you about. Either one of them is enough to explain what was wrong between us. Both of them together brought our friendship to an end. But to this day, thirty years later, I cannot for the life of me decide which of these two things really caused me to betray her. I repeat: ours was almost a perfect friendship. Or let me put it the other way round: ours was an imperfect friendship, but it was almost perfect.

I learned very soon in our relationship that Kathy was jealous. She did not like to think that I had anything she did not have. We would have great fun going out shopping but if I bought, say,

90

a dress for a party and she thought my dress was better than hers, she would start to say slightly unkind things about it. I could not understand this at all and even now it baffles me. She would be keen to come out with me to buy the dress. She would give me a lot of helpful advice while I was trying on the various dresses in the shops. Her advice would be very good. She would point out all sorts of things that I did not notice. She would even tell the shop assistants if she thought the price was too high. I can remember one occasion when she said this and, to my surprise, they knocked the price down so that I could afford to buy it. The trouble would come later. When we were actually going to the party and we were both dressed up and she was looking marvellous (for she was very beautiful) she would suddenly say, 'I think we were both wrong about that dress. It looks a bit cheap, doesn't it!'

At this, my self-confidence would start to melt away and I would be sorely tempted to turn round and go home. I was the kind of person who is easily hurt. It was easy to make me feel stupid or unwanted. My father used to make harsh comments on my appearance and I would run up to my room and think of ways of hurting him back. But it was impossible to hurt Dad. He only laughed at anything I said. I think I was the wrong kind of daughter for him. He wanted someone livelier and funnier. Perhaps he wanted someone like Kathy.

But if it was impossible ever to hit back at my father, it was just as impossible to hit back at Kathy. Once or twice I 'dropped' her. I told her I was too busy to see her. Or I told her I had to see another friend. All these lies hurt me because I had no other friend and so I was lonely. But they never hurt her. She just smiled sweetly and laughed and said she'd see me next week. And of course, within a week or so, I'd be on the phone asking her to come out. She never minded this. She never sulked at me and pretended that she was too busy. That was the marvellous thing about our friendship: we could always pick up where we left off.

The other problem was my mother. She thought Kathy was common. She thought Kathy had a bad influence over me. She even disliked Kathy's way of speaking. If I used certain phrases such as 'larking about' or 'having a laugh' Mum would get very angry. 'That's the kind of language you pick up from that girl. Don't bring it into this house, please.' Of course it was nonsense. Kathy spoke just as well as I did. She was much more confident than I was, so I think her speaking voice must have been better. And she was brave enough to say what she thought. There was nothing 'cheap' or 'common' about her. Not that I was anything special. Nor were my parents. But Mum disliked Kathy and looked down on her and kept on telling me to stop seeing her. If ever I invited her into the house, she would be angry and tell me off as soon as Kathy was gone.

Mother also had a fixed idea that Kathy would tell other people all sorts of terrible things about me, about my parents and about our house. Perhaps this was because Kathy was so friendly and talked with almost everyone. Perhaps even my Mum was jealous of this, because Mum was like me: backward at coming forward.

Thanks to Kathy I had a wonderful year at the Tech. As a result I looked forward to going out to work. If the Tech could be such fun, so could work! Perhaps I foolishly imagined that wherever I went I would meet another Kathy. But at the end of that wonderful year, two things happened that destroyed our friendship.

The students always celebrated the end of the college year with a fancy-dress ball. It was a big event. But as luck would have it, Kathy and I had made other arrangements for the day of the ball. We had booked to go to a theatre. We had talked for ages of going, and at last we had our tickets. For us this was a big event. It was a musical and our favourite singing star was in it. Then we realised that the students' dance was on the same day. It was a shame. But our hearts were set on the theatre.

Then Kathy came round to see me. Mother was in at the time, and I had to speak to her on the doorstep because Mum had just been having a go at me for seeing too much of Kathy. 'I don't want that girl coming in this house and snooping, and going around telling people what she sees!' So I told Kathy I couldn't invite her in because my Mum had a bad headache and we all had to keep quiet. Kathy didn't mind. She smiled and said she was sorry about my mother's bad head. I was sure she knew what had really happened. I was sure she knew what my mother thought of her. But she carried on smiling, and then she said: 'I'm sorry, but I can't come to the theatre with you after all. My brother's come home and he wants to take me to the fancy-dress ball at the college. I can't let him down. I hardly ever see him. And he'd bought the tickets before he told me about it.'

She must have seen the disappointment on my face. I couldn't believe that she would let me down. She knew how much I had looked forward to the theatre trip. We had talked about it together for months. Why should she suddenly prefer to please her brother? He was someone she hardly ever talked about. He was someone she hardly ever saw. He seemed to spend most of his time wandering around the country. Kathy had often said that her parents worried themselves silly about him, and that they were convinced he was getting into trouble. And now she was betraying me in order to please him.

Before she left she gave me her theatre ticket, saying, 'Take your Mum to see the show with you. I don't want paying for it. Tell her it's my treat.'

I was almost in tears by the time I had said goodbye to her and closed the door. My Mum could see how I was feeling and I told her what had happened. She was very kind and under-standing, and we talked a lot about friends and she even told me about friends she had had when she was a youngster.

'There aren't many friends you can trust,' said Mum. 'And I wouldn't trust that Kathy. There's something common about her. I always said there was.'

She made me promise that I would never see Kathy again. I agreed, and felt that was the least I could do by way of revenge for my disappoint-ment. I told myself that I would never so much as talk to Kathy if I saw her. Our relationship was at an end. I would never forgive her. I might even think of other ways to have my revenge on her.

Two months later I read in the newspaper that Kathy and her brother had been arrested on a charge of shoplifting and given a conditional discharge by the local magistrate. In other words, they had been found guilty and warned not to do it again. It was a very short story. Just a paragraph or two. It was Mum who noticed it and drew my attention to it. 'I told you what she's like. I knew it. I'm not surprised. She'll do worse than that before she's finished.'

I could not for one moment understand how Kathy could have done such a thing. It was so unlike her. I felt intensely sorry for her, and longed to see her to tell her that I still needed her friendship. In some strange way I felt that I was even to blame and that if I had carried on seeing her then this would not have happened. I even imagined that if I could see Kathy she would herself say that it would not have happened if I had still been her friend. But how could someone so lively and so confident and so interesting as Kathy, have done anything so stupid as to steal things from a shop? And get her name in the newspapers?

I decided that I would find an excuse for going round to see her. The next day, though, I was shopping in the High Street with my Mum and we both saw her. It was quite a long time since we had seen each other, and of course we were both finished now at the College and I had already started my first job. So perhaps we both looked very different. She certainly seemed much older and seemed to have lost her sparkle. She stopped to say hello to us but this time she seemed almost shy and embarrassed. Mum said, 'Hello, Kathy, nice to see you!' and smiled politely at her but carried on walking.

Kathy had stopped and looked at me as if to say, 'Can't we talk?'

I stopped and thought hard and unhappily about what I should say.

'Have you got a job yet, Sarah?'

I managed to reply, 'Yes. It's great. It's great fun!'

Mum was walking away from me. I wanted to stop and talk and begin all over again with Kathy. I hesitated. There was my promise to Mum; there was even that little part of me that wanted to have revenge on Kathy for the injury she had made me suffer. I knew that it was wrong to want revenge for something so slight, so unimportant. I knew that it was wrong of my mother to be so mean towards Kathy. After all, what's a little shoplifting between friends? But I hesitated a moment too long, for Kathy now turned away, saying, 'I'm glad you've got a job, Sarah. Hope it goes well for you.'

And she was gone. I had no chance to ask if she too was working. I had no chance to mend our friendship.

I caught up with Mum, who said, 'You did well to be like that with her. She's not your sort. Now you've got a job you can find new friends.'

But in fact it was a long time before I found another friend to amuse me and to cheer me up like Kathy had done. And to this day I still feel guilty because I did not go to her and cheer her up and amuse her when she would most have needed it.

from *Growing Pains* by Sarah Green
(adapted and abridged)

Oxford Street, London, in the 1940s

For Group Discussion

1 Why did Sarah's mother disapprove of Kathy?

2 Sarah says that the 'other' problem in her friendship with Kathy was her mother's attitude to Kathy. What does she say was the first problem?

3 Is it common for parents to disapprove of friends? What different reasons can there be for this disapproval?

4 What reason do you think Kathy would have given for the breakup of the friendship?

5 Is Sarah in any way to blame for what she did at the end of the story?

For Class Discussion

6 **Irony**

We often think and feel differently about an event after it has happened from the way we feel and think at the time. For example, we may be very excited about going to a party, but afterwards we may look back on it as something unimportant or even dull. This difference between how we feel now and how we felt then can be called *an irony* (or *ironic*). It is an irony that we now can hardly remember the party when at the time we could hardly think of anything else.

Is there any example of irony in either of these two stories?

PUNCTUATION:

The two stories in this Unit illustrate several points of punctuation that are worth noting:

1. **The Comma** is used in both stories as a way of marking off the name or identity of the person spoken to.

   For example: **Hello, Kathy, nice to see you.**
   Go on, Maubert, you're all right now.

   Other examples would be: **I told you, George, that I would not put up with that.**
   Good morning, gentlemen, it's good to see you.

2. **The apostrophe** is used in both stories to show words that have been abbreviated by leaving out letters.

   For example: **He'll soon be asking for help.** (*means* 'He will soon . . .')
   I've won! (*means* 'I have won!')

Re-read the first part of the first story. Write out the first ten examples of this use of the apostrophe and write out alongside them the full words that have been abbreviated.

3. **The apostrophe 's'** is used in both stories to show possession.

   For example: **Kathy's way of speaking**
   (*means* 'the way of speaking that belongs to Kathy')
   The students' dance
   (*means* 'the dance of, or organised by, the students')

Notice the way the apostrophe is moved after the *s* if the word is plural.

   For example: **The girl's home** (*means* 'the home of the girl – one girl')
   The girls' home (*means* 'the home of the girls – more than one girl')

For individual work   *Rewrite these sentences with any necessary changes of punctuation:*

1. 'Hello George I was hoping to see you' said Kay.

2. George replied 'Its good to see you too.'

3. 'Are you going to the students dance' asked Kay.

4. 'Thats what I was going to ask you said George. 'Are you going?'

5. Its a possibility Kay said.

6. 'i was planning to invite you. Its Berts birthday and i thought we could make a party with him and elsie.

7. That sounds like a great idea said kay but i'm not sure that my Dadll let me go.

8. Ill ask him said George.

9. Do you think thats a good idea? said Kay.

10. He knows me. Were old friends, said George.

Note *that if you use a question mark you do not need a comma as well.*

For example: **'Do you know me?' he asked.**   *Not:* **'Do you know me?,' he asked.**

QUESTIONS *on the two stories: for individual work*

1. When Maubert first sees André Chamson at the river bank, what does he decide to do?

2. What does André decide to do when he first sees Maubert swimming?

3. Why do you think André decides to let Maubert get out of the water?

4. Maubert asks, 'Why do you hate me?' What do you think is the real answer to this question?

5. At the end of the story, André says there was 'something of regret' in his decision to treat Maubert as an enemy. Why do you think he feels any regret?

6. Sarah Green says that her friendship with Kathy was not perfect. What is the first reason she gives for this?

7. How does Sarah get on with her father?

8. What does it mean when she says, 'And a little bit of her character rubbed off on me'? (end of paragraph 2)

9. What do you think is the best thing about Kathy's character as it is shown in this story?

10. Sarah thought that Kathy was jealous, and also that her mother was jealous. According to Sarah, what were the things that they were jealous of?

11. Is there any clue in the story to suggest that Sarah was jealous? If so, what was she jealous of?

12. What part did the parents play (in both stories) in causing the young people to act as they did towards each other?

13. When Sarah met Kathy in the High Street she 'hesitated' because she could not decide what to do. Was there any point in the first story when André hesitated because he did not know what to do?

14. André ends his story by saying he felt regret that now they had to be enemies again. Copy out one sentence from the second story that shows that Sarah also felt regret when the friendship came to an end.

15. Who do you think is most to blame for the way Sarah's and Kathy's friendship comes to an end? Give your reasons.

Oxford Street, London, in the 1940s

Role play . . .

Discuss further the various reasons why the characters in these stories become friends or enemies, and why they suddenly change from one to the other.

Then interview one member of the class as if he or she is one of the characters and the rest of you are, say, writers who are keen to write a story about what has happened and want to know everything about it.

Ask a great range of questions, going beyond what is told in the stories you have been reading. Ask about their earlier lives, and about their likes and dislikes, their attitudes to life in general, the way they feel now about what happened, and so on. Build up a complete picture of each of the characters.

Then ask another student to take on the role of another character in the same story – perhaps one of the parents.

and improvisation

Make up a scene that is not in either of the stories but involves the same characters.

For example: improvise a scene where André meets Maubert after the events of the story. Perhaps it is in a store where they have both found part-time jobs while they are still at school or college. It is their tea-break.

Or improvise a scene where Kathy meets Sarah after the events of the story. It is a Saturday morning and they have both walked into the same cafe for a coffee.

Group Discussion

A group of students discussed the various things that can cause friendships to break up.

This is part of their report:

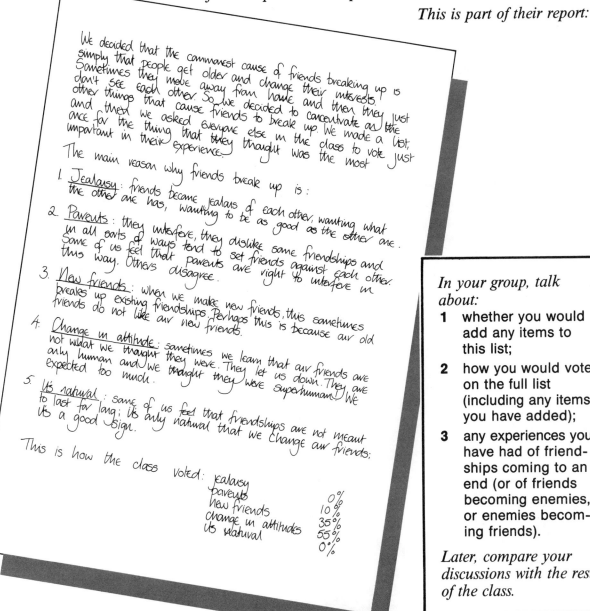

We decided that the commonest cause of friends breaking up is simply that people get older and change their interests. Sometimes they move away from home and then they just don't see each other. So we decided to concentrate on the other things that cause friends to break up. We made a list, and then we asked everyone else in the class to vote just once for the thing that they thought was the most important in their experience.

The main reason why friends break up is:

1. <u>Jealousy</u>: friends become jealous of each other, wanting what the other one has, wanting to be as good as the other one.

2. <u>Parents</u>: they interfere, they dislike some friendships and in all sorts of ways tend to set friends against each other. Some of us feel that parents are right to interfere in this way. Others disagree.

3. <u>New friends</u>: when we make new friends, this sometimes breaks up existing friendships. Perhaps this is because our old friends do not like our new friends.

4. <u>Change in attitude</u>: sometimes we learn that our friends are not what we thought they were. They let us down. They are only human and we thought they were superhuman! We expected too much.

5. <u>It's natural</u>: some of us feel that friendships are not meant to last for long; it's only natural that we change our friends; it's a good sign.

This is how the class voted:
Jealousy	0%
Parents	10%
New friends	35%
Change in attitudes	55%
It's natural	0%

In your group, talk about:

1 whether you would add any items to this list;

2 how you would vote on the full list (including any items you have added);

3 any experiences you have had of friendships coming to an end (or of friends becoming enemies, or enemies becoming friends).

Later, compare your discussions with the rest of the class.

WRITING

*Write a **story** on the theme of friendship. Perhaps draw on your own experiences and on the experiences of others.*

*Or write a **report** on the theme of friendship, referring to the stories you have just read in class and to the improvisations and discussions, and including experiences of your own.*

10 Fear

drawn for a radio play, The Green Man *by Keiren Phelps*

Psychology is the study of the mind. In this extract, a psychologist looks at some of the things that frighten us, and wonders whether fear may be useful.

Why Be Frightened?

There are some things that frighten everyone. We are all frightened of things that we know to be dangerous, such as certain kinds of animals. When we are growing up, we learn very quickly to keep away from such dangers. When we go to the zoo for the first time, we may need to be told that we must not leave mother or father, but we need very little telling about the serious dangers. We are not tempted to climb the fence that separates us from the tigers, or to find the door that leads us into the snakes' house.

Fear is very helpful. If we had no sense of fear, we would be dangerous not only to others but also to ourselves. We would not last very long. We would run wildly into a road full of traffic. We would jump off the tops of buildings. We would keep on playing with fire. We would destroy ourselves. So fear keeps us alive.

This gives rise to a number of questions. For example, do we have to be taught to be afraid? Or is fear something that needs no teaching? The usual way of answering this is to say that we have a basic sense of fear, but that we learn from others the actual objects of our fear. In other words, children (and adults) can be taught to be afraid. And they can be taught differently. Some people are scared of heights. Some people are scared of people who look different. Some people are scared of big cities. And so on.

So, although fear helps to keep us alive, we can have too much fear. In fact, it is possible to have so much fear that we can be destroyed by fear. We can be afraid, for example, to defend ourselves, or to leave home, or to go out in the dark, or to ask the way. In such cases, we have learned the wrong things. We have allowed our own natural fear to get out of hand.

Another way of saying this is that our natural instincts are controlled by our social experience. We learn from others and what we learn may in fact harm us. We become timid. Our nervous system tries too hard to look after itself.

For example, a fear of heights is both natural and useful. It stops us from climbing onto the roof and jumping off. It makes us careful when we climb a ladder. But at the same time, such a fear can get out of hand. We may become so frightened that we cannot climb any ladder at all, no matter how safe it may be, and no matter how much we need to climb it. Indeed we can become too scared to climb anything – even the stairs!

Also, we can be scared of something even though we know it cannot possibly harm us. We can be scared by Dracula in the films, for example, even though we know he is only in a film and that the film will end in fifty minutes or so. Or we may be scared by Frankenstein's creature, even though we know he cannot leap out of the pages of the book and grab us by the throat. Does this kind of fear help us at all? Does it serve a useful purpose?

The Psychology of Fear, by Ursula Johnson, (adapted)

For Discussion

1   What does the writer think is the main way in which fear helps us?

2   In what way can fear be harmful?

3   What is the main point made in the last paragraph?

4   What would be your answer to the writer's final question?

When I am frightened . . .

This is part of a student's account of the things that frighten him. It is given here with the sentences in the wrong order.

Work out the right order. Just write down the numbers 1 to 10 underneath each other, and then write down the appropriate letter at the side of each number.

Then compare your answers with each other, reading out the sentences aloud in the order you have worked out.

A At such times, I do all sorts of silly things to avoid being sent into the darkness.

B I am also scared of looking a fool.

C Sometimes, for instance, I pretend my family are out until late, so that I can stay longer where I am.

D I can remember going to parties, for example, and being too scared to go home because of the dark.

E Let me say to begin with, that too many things frighten me.

F For example, I hardly ever answer questions in class, just in case I give a silly answer.

G But I know this is stupid, because in the end, I still have to go home and brave the darkness, and when I do it is even later and even darker!

H I know it scares most people, but it scares me too much.

I I will do anything and everything to make sure people do not laugh at me and think me stupid.

J The dark scares me almost to death.

Group Work on *'Why be frightened?'*

Work on the following questions in pairs or small groups.

Subheadings should give a clear summary of what is written. Re-read the extract and then choose the best subheadings from the three possible ones given.

1 For paragraph 1
   a) Fear is helpful.
   b) Everyone feels fear.
   c) Animals cause fear.

2 For paragraph 3
   a) Fear keeps us alive.
   b) We all fear something.
   c) We learn what to fear.

3 For paragraph 5
   a) Fear can be bad for you!
   b) Never be afraid!
   c) Fear is good for you!

4 For paragraph 6
   a) Dracula is bad for you!
   b) Fear can be foolish.
   c) Fear is foolish.

And which of these would be the best subheading for the whole extract?

5 a) Some questions about fear.
   b) Strange things about fear.
   c) Fear – its good and bad sides.

True or False?

Which of these statements is correct according to the passage? Just write TRUE or FALSE.

6 Fear is a natural human instinct.

7 Some people are afraid of nothing.

8 Some people are afraid of too many things.

9 It is silly to be scared of heights.

10 It is possible to be destroyed by fear.

11 There is no need to be afraid of anything.

12 We cannot be taught to be afraid of anything.

13 The writer thinks it is silly to be scared of films or books.

14 The writer thinks there is no point in watching films about Dracula or Frankenstein.

15 The writer thinks we should think hard about the things that frighten us.

For Discussion

16 Make a note on your own of the three things that most frighten you (leaving out, for the moment, anything in films and books). Then compare your list with each other, and make up a new list of the three things that most frighten all of your group.

17 Can you think of any times when being frightened has helped you?

18 How do you think you have learned to be afraid of the things that frighten you?

19 What books or films have frightened you? Why?

20 Do you think you learn anything from books or films that frighten you?

Later, compare your answers with the rest of the class.

Frightened of being frightened

This is part of another student's account of the things that frighten her. It is given here in three sections. Read and talk about each section separately.

Section 1

The trouble with me is that I sometimes seem to be afraid of fear itself. I become more frightened because I'm frightened. A good example is my fear of examinations. Sometimes I can go into an exam and not feel anything. It's no more than an ordinary day's work. Then another time I start to get scared. Perhaps I wake up scared, and don't know why, and then I suddenly remember: exams today! In other words, the fear comes before the thought. The feeling comes first! And then nothing I do can calm me down. I try to say to myself, 'Julia, don't worry! You've taken exams before, and you've lived to tell the tale. And you'll survive this too...'

But it's no use. I can't stop being frightened, and because I cannot stop it, the feeling gets worse.

I honestly cannot think of a time when my fears just faded away. If I'm on my own in a house and I hear a strange noise upstairs, I never have the courage to go upstairs and look. I sit as quiet as a mouse and pretend to watch the television, or pretend to do my homework, but really I am just sitting waiting for the terrible something (whatever it is) to happen. Nothing takes my fear away. I am never able to think it out of my head. I am imprisoned by my fear until, of course, my family come home. Then I can hardly remember my fear!

There's one thing I have never had the courage to do. I cannot watch a horror film on my own. I have to be in company, and I have to be sure that the company will not leave before I do!

For Discussion

1 What does the writer mean when she says, 'the fear comes before the thought'?

2 What does she mean when she says, 'I am imprisoned by my fear'?

3 Do you share either of the fears she mentions here?

4 How do you think she could learn or be helped to overcome the fear of either exams or of watching horror films on her own?

Section 2 Cloze Test

The next section of her writing is given here with some of the words missing. Working in pairs or small groups, read it together and choose ONE word for each space. Just write the numbers 1 to 10 underneath each other and then write the words you have chosen alongside the numbers.

On one occasion I had to get -(**1**)- for a history exam. It was Tuesday evening and the -(**2**)- was on Wednesday afternoon. I got out my history exercise books and -(**3**)- to revise my notes. Then I started to think about the exams. Then I started to remember how much I -(**4**)- exams. Soon I realised that I not only hated them but also feared them. I became so -(**5**)- about them that I found it difficult to revise my history notes. I came out in a cold -(**6**)-. I could not stop worrying about the exam, and the exam room, and me sitting in the exam room. It got to be so -(**7**)- I could hardly read the history notes at all. Then I got worried because this -(**8**)- I would not know my notes enough to do well in the exams. I realise now that I could have -(**9**)- myself by asking my Mum to go through the history notes with me, and by chatting with her about my fears. I think that that is the best way to -(**10**)- fear: talk about it!

Now re-read the passage with your answers.

drawn for a radio play, Death!, *by Keiren Phelps*

103

I suppose the thing that in general I am afraid of is the unknown. In a way, fear of the dark is fear of the unknown. But to be fair, I must add that knowing something does not necessarily mean that I am any the less scared of it. For example, I am scared of the water. I hate swimming. I am always sure that I am going to drown. And this is not because I cannot swim - strangely enough, I can. But I saw an accident some years ago in a swimming pool, and ever since then I have been scared of the water.

In case you think I am scared of everything, I must add very quickly that I am not. To give just one example, I am not scared of flying: I love it.

I sometimes wonder where my fears come from. Not all of them can be explained away so easily as my fear of the water. Maybe we pick up some of our fears from the things that frighten others. Maybe I am afraid of exams because so many other people are, and they have given me the same feeling. Maybe people have said to me, 'Don't be afraid...', and that has made me scared stiff!

If you ask me what is my greatest fear, I would have to think long and carefully. Some of my fears are important to me, but they do not come to me very often. My greatest fear must be the one that is always with me. I think it must be a fear of not being wanted or liked by anyone. I do not want everyone to like me, but I must have someone who does. I remember once going on a camping holiday with a small group of friends and in the middle of the holiday I realised that none of them was a friend at all. I did not really like any of them. And, just as bad, none of them seemed to like me. I got more and more depressed and could hardly wait for the 'holiday' to come to an end. In fact we were only away for five days, but those five days seemed to last for ever!

Julia Martins (extract)

For Discussion

1 Can you think of other examples to show that it is not always the unknown that frightens us?

2 Would you agree that telling people not to be afraid can make them afraid?

3 Julia's greatest fear is 'not being wanted or liked by anyone'. Do you think this is a reasonable fear to have? Do you think it is a useful one?

4 Suggest a short subheading for each of the four paragraphs.

PUNCTUATION:

Rewrite these sentences with commas *used where necessary.*

1. While we were on holiday together Janice Kate Anne and I seemed at first to get on very well.
2. Soon however this changed.
3. We started to sulk quarrel show off and argue.

Rewrite these sentences with apostrophes *used where necessary.*

4. Kate didnt like Anne.
5. Kates bad temper annoyed all of us.
6. Theres no one so bad tempered as Kate.

Rewrite these sentences with commas, apostrophes and speech marks *used where necessary.*

7. Janice said Ive had enough.
8. So have I I said.
9. Since we all seem to have had enough said Anne perhaps we should all go home.
10. Kate added thats a marvellous idea!

The apostrophe 's'

In the last Unit the difference was stressed between the following:

> **the boy's team** (*meaning* 'the team of one boy')
> **the boys' team** (*meaning* 'the team of more than one boy')

Notice, though, that some words break this rule. These are words that form their plural without adding an s.

Examples are: **the child's home / the children's home**
(the apostrophe stays in front of the s)

the man's or woman's home / the men's or women's home
(the apostrophe stays in front of the s)

Notice also that one of the commonest mistakes in writing is to place the apostrophe after the wrong word. It goes after the word that has or possesses something, *not* after the thing that is possessed.

For example: **He sold his friend's books.**
not **He sold his friends books'.**

He spoke to her father's lawyers.
not **He spoke to her fathers laywers'.**

Revision

Rewrite these sentences with any necessary changes of punctuation.

1. They thought that there wasnt time for reading the standard.
2. They decided instead to visit the upper school library and read the daily telegraph.
3. They found a news story about recent riots in paris france.

4 Theres troubles everywhere said Maria.

5 Anne pointed out That makes my familys troubles seem unimportant.

6 If you read the newspapers they always cheer you up said Maria.

7 i cant say they cheer me up replied Anne.

8 Heres an article about womens place in modern society said Albert.

9 What does it say asked Maria.

10 It says that woman's place is in the home! said Anne.

11 Dont you believe it, said Maria.

12 I dont said anne.

FOR FURTHER DISCUSSION AND WRITING

Working in pairs or small groups, talk about possible ways of planning and writing an essay on the different things that make people afraid.

In your essay you might perhaps refer to and quote from one or two of the texts in this Unit.

A possible way of planning your essay would be:

Section 1: different things that frighten different people, excluding for the moment your own personal fears;

Section 2: your own fears, with stories from your own experience;

Section 3: possible theories to explain:
a) in general, why people experience fear;
b) in particular, why you yourself experience your own personal fears, including the question 'is fear useful?'

11 Dramatic Conflict

Drama revolves around characters whose aims or motives come into some kind of conflict with each other. Drama can take many different forms, and most of us spend a fair part of our lives just watching dramas.

For example, how many students in your class have seen any of the following?

Stage play, stage musical, opera, ballet, pantomime, film, TV play, TV serial

*And how many of you have heard a **radio play?***

Also, which of these have most students seen (or heard) most of?

The texts in this Unit concentrate on the straight (i.e. non musical) play, both scripted and improvised.

from Hobson's Choice *directed by David Lean, 1953*

Hobson's Choice

The play is set in Salford, Lancashire, in 1850. Willie Mossop *makes shoes for Henry Hobson's shoe shop. He is brilliant at his job. Maggie, the boss's daughter, realises just how brilliant he is . . .*

Maggie: (*She closes door and moves to trap, which she raises.*) Willie, come here.

In a moment Willie appears, and stops half-way up.

Willie: Yes, Miss Maggie?

Maggie: Come up, and put the trap down; I want to talk to you.

He comes, reluctantly.

Willie: We're very busy in the cellar.

Maggie points to trap. He closes it.

Maggie: Show me your hands, Willie.
Willie: They're dirty. (*He holds them out hesitatingly.*)
Maggie: Yes, they're dirty, but they're clever. They can shape the leather like no other man's that ever came into the shop. Who taught you, Willie? (*She retains his hands.*)
Willie: Why, Miss Maggie, I learnt my trade here.
Maggie: Hobson's never taught you to make boots the way you do.
Willie: I've had no other teacher.
Maggie (*dropping his hands*): And needed none. You're a natural born genius at making boots. It's a pity you're a natural fool at all else.
Willie: I'm not much good at owt but leather, and that's a fact.
Maggie: When are you going to leave Hobson's?
Willie: Leave Hobson's? I – I thought I gave satisfaction?
Maggie: Don't you want to leave?
Willie: Not me. I've been at Hobson's all my life, and I'm not leaving till I'm made.
Maggie: I said you were a fool.
Willie: Then I'm a loyal fool.
Maggie: Don't you want to get on, Will Mossop? You heard what Mrs Hepworth said. You know the wages you get and you know the wages a bootmaker like you could get in one of the big shops in Manchester.
Willie: Nay, I'd be feared to go in them fine places.
Maggie: What keeps you here? Is it the – the people?
Willie: I dunno what it is. I'm used to being here.
Maggie: Do you know what keeps this business on its legs? Two things; one's the good boots you make that sell themselves, the others the bad boots other people make and I sell. We're a pair, Will Mossop.
Willie: You're a wonder in the shop, Miss Maggie.
Maggie: And you're a marvel in the workshop. Well?
Willie: Well, what?
Maggie: It seems to me to point one way.
Willie: What way is that?
Maggie: You're leaving me to do the work, my lad.
Willie: I'll be getting back to my stool, Miss Maggie. (*Moves to trap*).
Maggie (*stopping him*): You'll go back when I've done with you. I've watched you for a long time and everything I've seen, I've liked. I think you'll do for me.
Willie: What way, Miss Maggie?
Maggie: Will Mossop, you're my man. Six months I've counted on you and it's got to come out some time.
Willie: But I never –
Maggie: I know you never, or it 'ud not be left to me to do the job like this.

Willie:	I'll – I'll sit down. (*He sits in the arm-chair, mopping his brow.*) I'm feeling queer-like. What dost want me for?
Maggie:	To invest in. You're a business idea in the shape of a man.
Willie:	I've got not head for business at all.
Maggie:	But I have. My brain and your hands 'ull make a working partnership.
Willie	(*getting up, relieved*): Partnership! Oh, that's a different thing. I thought you were axing me to wed you.
Maggie:	I am.
Willie:	Well by gum! And you the master's daughter.
Maggie:	Maybe that's why, Will Mossop. Maybe I've had enough of father, and you're as different from him as any man I know.
Willie:	It's a bit awkward-like.
Maggie:	And you don't help me any, lad. What's awkward about it?
Willie:	You talking to me like this.
Maggie:	I'll tell you something, Will. It's a poor sort of woman who'll stay lazy when she sees her best chance slipping from her. A Salford life's too near the bone to lose things through fear of speaking out.
Willie:	I'm your best chance?
Maggie:	You are that, Will.
Willie:	Well by gum! I never thought of this.
Maggie:	Think of it now.
Willie:	I am doing. Only the blow's a bit too sudden to think very clear. I've a great respect for you, Miss Maggie. You're a shapely body, and you're a masterpiece at selling in the shop, but when it comes to marrying, I'm bound to tell you that I'm none in love with you.
Maggie:	Wait till you're asked. I want your hand in mine and your word for it that you'll go through life with me for the best we can get out of it.
Willie:	We'd not get much without there's love between us, lass.
Maggie:	I've got the love all right.
Willie:	Well I've not, and that's honest.
Maggie:	We'll get along without.
Willie:	You're desperate set on this. It's a puzzle to me all ways. What 'ud your father say?
Maggie:	He'll say a lot, and he can say it. It'll make no difference to me.
Willie:	Much better not upset him. It's not worth while.
Maggie:	I'm the judge of that. You're going to wed me, Will.
Willie:	Oh, nay, I'm not. Really I can't do that, Maggie. I can see that I'm disturbing your arrangements like, but I'll be obliged if you'll put this notion from you.
Maggie:	When I make arrangements, my lad, they're not made for upsetting.
Willie:	What makes it so desperate awkward is that I'm tokened.
Maggie:	You're what?
Willie:	I'm tokened to Ada Figgins.
Maggie:	Then you'll get loose and quick. Who's Ada Figgins? Do I know her?
Willie:	I'm the lodger at her mother's.
Maggie:	The scheming hussy. It's not that sandy girl who brings your dinner?
Willie:	She's golden-haired is Ada. Aye, she'll be here soon.
Maggie:	And so shall I. I'll talk to Ada. I've seen her and I know the breed. Ada's the helpless sort.

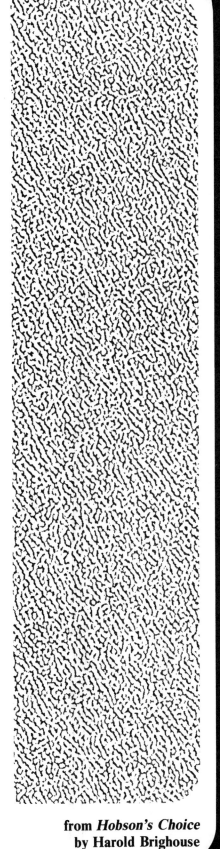

**from *Hobson's Choice*
by Harold Brighouse**

109

Washington Square

Catherine *is rich, having inherited a lot of money when her mother died. Her father,* Dr Sloper, *is very wealthy, and when he dies she will inherit his fortune. She is pleasant but shy, and falls head over heels in love with a handsome young stranger,* Morris Townsend. *Dr Sloper believes that Morris is only after her money and he tries to persuade Catherine not to see him again.*

The play is set in New York in the mid-nineteenth century.

film stills from *The Heiress*, adapted from *Washington Square* and directed by William Wyler, 1949

Dr Sloper Tell me something, Catherine.

Catherine What is it, father?

Dr Sloper Do you wish to make me very happy?

Catherine I should like to. But I am afraid I can't.

Dr Sloper You can if you will. It all depends on you.

Catherine Is it to give up Morris?

Dr Sloper Yes, it is to give him up.

Catherine That would make me very unhappy.

Dr Sloper I have no doubt that you are very unhappy just now. But it is better to be unhappy for a few months and get over it, than to be unhappy for the rest of your life.

Catherine Yes. But Morris cannot make me unhappy.

Dr Sloper I am sure he will. Have you no faith in my experience? In my concern for you? Do you think I do not know men better than you do?

Catherine Yes, Father, but you do not know Morris as I do. He is not false; he is not cruel.

Dr Sloper Then you think I know nothing? You think I am stupid? You think you know more of men than I do?

Catherine But Morris loves me. I cannot believe he could do me harm.

Dr Sloper I do not ask you to believe it. I just ask you to do as I tell you, and to trust me.

Catherine But what has he done? What do you know?

Dr Sloper He has never done anything. That is the whole point. He does nothing. He is an idler! He just walks around the city looking for a fortune. And now he has found one.

Catherine Oh, father, you must not insult him. I beg you.

Dr Sloper [*Losing patience*] Very well, then. Do as you wish.

Catherine You mean I can see him again?

Dr Sloper Yes. See him again.

Catherine And you will forgive me?

Dr Sloper Certainly not.

Catherine I wish only to see him once. To tell him to wait.

Dr Sloper To wait for what?

Catherine To wait till you know him better. Till you give your consent.

Dr Sloper Don't tell him any such nonsense. I know him already, and I will never give my consent.

Catherine We can wait a long time.

Dr Sloper Of course, you can wait till I die, if you like.

Catherine I would rather not marry at all. I wish to be faithful to you, Father. I wish to be a true and faithful daughter. But I also wish to be true to Morris. He loves me, and I love him.

Dr Sloper If you love me, then you will give him up. It is as simple as that.

Catherine But I think that if you would only let Morris speak to you, you would come to like him. You would come to understand him.

Dr Sloper I understand him well enough already. I shall never speak to him again.

Catherine But why do you dislike him so much? And why do you not trust me?

Dr Sloper Tell Morris Townsend one thing. Tell him this: if you marry him, I will disinherit you. I will not leave you anything at all. See what he thinks about that.

Catherine It will make no difference to him, Father.

Dr Sloper For your sake, my child, I hope you are right. But I know you are wrong . . .

[*Later, Dr Sloper takes Catherine on holiday to Europe, hoping that she will forget Morris. She does not. At last he realises that nothing can make her change her mind. He tells her again that he will disinherit her, but this time he promises he will do nothing else to discourage her. She tells this to Morris.*]

Catherine In time he may change his mind. We must pray for that, Morris.

Morris He insults me. He treats me as someone worse than a criminal. A fortune-hunter!

Catherine He does not know you.

Morris It is a great insult.

Catherine We must bear these things together. That's what we must do. We have each other. We must help each other.

Morris But he will not be the only one. Others will say what he says.

Catherine But what difference will that make?

Morris It is easy for you to say that. But how do you think it will be for me? People will say what your father says. They'll look at us and whisper about us, 'He married her for her money, like her father says!'

Catherine No. No one will say that. No one who knows you!

Morris There is only one way of stopping such things. And you must help me.

Catherine I will do anything. You know I will.

Morris I ask you one thing only: do not make a scene!

Catherine A scene! Do I make scenes?

Morris All women do.

Catherine I don't. I only want to help you.

Morris I have to go away. On business. I must make my fortune, Catherine, so that nobody can ever accuse me of marrying you in order to share your fortune.

Catherine	But where are you going? You must take me with you.
Morris	Take you with me – on business?
Catherine	But your business is to be with me.
Morris	No. It wouldn't be right. I have to go first to New Orleans. There are terrible dangers there.
Catherine	But what does that matter to me?
Morris	It is a nest of yellow fever. I could not possibly put you at risk.
Catherine	If you can go to New Orleans, then I can go. I am as strong as you are, Morris, and not in the least afraid of any fever.
Morris	You said you wouldn't make a scene. I call this a scene.
Catherine	You won't go! Promise me you will not go.
Morris	I must see to my business – to my career!
Catherine	But we do not need money. I already have all the money we need.
Morris	I refuse to live on your money.
Catherine	But you never spoke like this before. You are going to leave me, Morris.
Morris	For a little while. Till you are reasonable again.
Catherine	But, Morris, I have given up everything for you.
Morris	My dear Catherine, you have given up too much, that is why you must let me go to make my own fortune. Then I will come back to you.
Catherine	[*Believing now that she will never see him again*] What has happened? What have I done? What has changed you?
Morris	I will write you a letter. That is the best way. And then later I will come back to you. I swear it, Catherine. When my fortune is made, I will come back and we will be together always. [*He goes.*]

adapted from *Washington Square* by Henry James

For Group Discussion

1   Why does Dr Sloper not trust Morris?
2   What other method might he have used to discourage Catherine from trusting Morris?
3   Why did Dr Sloper fail to get Catherine to change her mind?
4   Will Morris ever come back to her?

Now compare your answers with the rest of the class.

Night Must Fall

Mrs Bramson *is a rich invalid, confined to a wheelchair, and living in a remote part of Essex. She is dictatorial with the servants and is used to having her own way. In this scene she has sent for a young man,* Dan, *who works as a page at a hotel, and who has made one of her maids,* Dora, *pregnant. She intends to tell him that he must now look after Dora and marry her.*

Earlier in the scene, she has read in the newspapers of a series of murders of young women in the district. But she thinks no more about these when Dan comes to meet her.

Mrs Bramson (*sternly*): Now, young man, what about Dora? I –

Dan: Wait a minute ... (*putting his hat on the table and going to her*). Are you sure you're comfortable like that? Don't you think, Mrs Bramson, you ought to be facin' ... a wee bit more this side, towards the sun more, eh? (*He moves her chair round till she is in the centre of the room, facing the sun-room.*) You're looking pale you know. I am sorry. Excuse rudeness ... Another thing, Mrs Bramson – you don't mind me sayin' it, do you? – but you ought to have a rug, you know. This October weather's very treacherous.

Mrs Bramson: Pale? Did you say pale?

Dan: Washed out. The minute I saw you just now, I said to myself – now there's a lady that's got a lot to contend with.

Mrs Bramson: Oh ... Well, I have. Nobody knows it better than me.

Dan: No, I'm sure ... Oh, it must be terrible to watch everybody else striding up and down enjoying everything, and to see everybody tasting the fruit – I'm sorry ... I didn't ha' ought to say that.

Mrs Bramson: But it's true! As true as you are my witness, and nobody else – now look here, about that girl –

Dan: Excuse me a minute ... Would you mind sayin' something?

Mrs Bramson: What d'you want me to say?

Dan: Yes ...

Mrs Bramson: Yes. What?

Dan: There's a funny twitching in your neck when you talk – very slight, of course – nerves, I expect – but I hope your doctor knows all about it ... D'you mind if I ask what your ailments are?

Mrs Bramson: ... Hadn't you better sit down?

Dan (*sitting*): Thank you.

Mrs Bramson: Well, I have the most terrible palpitations. I –

Dan: Palpitation? But the way you get about!

Mrs Bramson: Oh?

Dan: It's a pretty bad thing to have, you know. D'you know that nine women out of ten in your position'd be just sittin' down giving way?

Mrs Bramson: Would they?

Dan: Yes, they would! I do know, as a matter of fact. I've known people with palpitations. Somebody very close to me ... (*after a pause*) They're dead now ...

Mrs Bramson: Oh!

Dan: My mother, as a matter of fact ... I can just remember her.

Mrs Bramson: Oh?

Dan: She died when I was six. I know that, because my dad died two years before that.

Mrs Bramson: Oh.

Dan (*studying her*): As a matter o'fact –

Mrs Bramson: Yes?

Dan: Oh, no, it's a daft thing – It's only fancy I suppose ... but ... you remind me a bit of her.

Mrs Bramson:	Of your mother? Oh . . .	**Mrs Bramson:**	I think you deserve better – (*Sharply*) Talking of the right thing, what about Dora?
Dan:	Have you got a son?		
Mrs Bramson:	I haven't anybody at all.	**Dan:**	Oh, I know I'm to blame; I'm not much of a chap, but I'd put things straight like a shot if I had any money . . . But, you see, I work at the Tallboys, get thirty bob a week, with tips – but listen to me botherin' you with my worries and rubbish the state you're in . . . well!
Dan:	Oh . . . But I don't like to talk too much about my mother. Makes me feel . . . sort of sad . . . She had the same eyes very wide apart as you, and – and the same very good hands.		
Mrs Bramson:	Oh? . . . and the same palpitations?		
Dan:	And the same palpitations. You don't mind me talking about your health, do you?	**Mrs Bramson:**	No! I can stand it. I've taken a liking to you.
Mrs Bramson:	No.	**Dan:**	Well . . . That's very kind of you, Mrs Bramson.
Dan:	Well, d'you know you ought to get used to letting *other* people do things for you?	**Mrs Bramson:**	It's the way you talked about your mother. That's what it was.
		Dan:	Was it?
Mrs Bramson	(*a great truth dawning on her*): Yes!	**Mrs Bramson:**	Have you got to go back?
Dan:	You ought to be *very* careful.	**Dan:**	Now? Well no, not really . . . I've finished my duty now I done that errand, and this is my half-day.
Mrs Bramson:	Yes! (*After a pause, eyeing him as he smiles at her.*) You're a funny boy to be a page-boy.		
		Mrs Bramson	(*imperiously*): Stay to lunch.
Dan (*shyly*):	D'you think so?	**Dan:**	Well – I don't like to impose myself –
Mrs Bramson:	Well, now I come to talk to you, you seem so much better class – I mean, you know so much of the world.	**Mrs Bramson:**	In the kitchen, of course.
		Dan:	Oh, I know –
		Mrs Bramson:	There's plenty of food! Stay to lunch!
Dan:	I've knocked about a good bit, you know. Never had any advantages, but I always tried to do the right thing.	**Dan:**	Well – I don't know . . . all right, so long as you let me help a bit this morning . . .

abridged from *Night Must Fall* by Emlyn Williams

film still from Night Must Fall *directed by Karel Reisz, 1964*

For Discussion

1 Mrs Bramson's intentions when the scene begins are to be severe with Dan and to make him do the 'right thing' by Dora. What stops her from achieving this?

2 What are Dan's intentions when he meets Mrs Bramson?

3 What are the main things the audience learn about Dan in this scene?

4 When the audience know something that the characters in a drama do not know, it is called *dramatic irony*. For example, there is dramatic irony when the audience know that X has put poison in Y's drink but Y does not know it. Is there any dramatic irony in this scene?

QUESTIONS *on all three plays*

Before you answer these questions, you should re-read all three excerpts, working together in small groups.

Then talk about the questions below and write down your answers individually.

1   What is the first thing that Maggie says (in *Hobson's Choice*) that shows she is used to giving orders?

2   Maggie tells Willie that he is a 'natural fool'. Give two pieces of evidence from the scene to show that he probably is.

3   What evidence is there in the scene to suggest that in the end Willie probably will marry Maggie?

4   What is Catherine's intention in the scene from *Washington Square* between her father and herself?

5   Why does Dr Sloper ask Catherine to tell Morris that her father will disinherit her if she marries Morris?

6   Explain exactly what it is that suggests Morris does NOT love Catherine.

7   How do you think Dr Sloper will behave towards Catherine when he learns that Morris has left her?

8   In what different ways (in *Night Must Fall*) does Dan flatter Mrs Bramson?

9   What evidence is there in this scene that Dan is a liar?

10 What evidence is there in this scene that Mrs Bramson is used to giving people orders?

11 What is the main similarity between the extracts from *Washington Square* and *Hobson's Choice*?

12 What is the main similarity between all three extracts?

Structured Improvisation

Missing

These are notes for an improvised drama involving four characters. The notes are in two separate sections: the first (given here), for the whole class including the characters; the second (given in the Teacher's Book), for the whole class and for each individual character in turn.

| Characters: | **Mother** | **Father** |
| | **Daughter** | **Son's friend** (male) |

N.B. The characters should be given the actual first names of the actors themselves. Also give a name to the son.

Basic situation for everyone (class and characters included):

Father is a local businessman, owning a greengrocery. He is well off. Mother works occasionally at the shop but spends most of her time looking after the house and the family. The daughter is taking A-levels at school and is planning to go on later to university. The son and his friend are taking a course in business management at a technical college.

Three days ago the son disappeared. After leaving college he went home, had dinner and went out to visit a friend at his house. He has not been seen or heard of since. The police have been informed, but they have found no trace of him. Apparently he did not get to his friend's house, though the friend had been expecting him and waited in for him all evening.

The scene that is to be improvised takes place at the family home. It is early evening, and the parents have invited the friend to come and talk to them about their son, hoping that he may be able to tell them something to explain his disappearance.

ROLE PLAY

After the structured improvisation, interview each of the characters in turn as if you are, say, social workers trying to sort out what has happened and why.

Ask a great range of questions to build up a complete picture of the family and of the son – their histories, their attitudes, their lives, their interests, and so on.

Later, repeat the interviews with different players.

IDEAS

Ideas for drama can come from anywhere, including personal experiences and things overheard. Here, for example, is how one playwright, Ray Jenkins, *got the idea for one of his plays:*

One very hot day, ages ago, my younger brother suddenly asked my mother for a button-collar shirt. Point-blank – while she was doing the washing. He was a quiet boy, and for him to ask for something out of the blue like that was unusual to say the least. But he did – and unfortunately at that time my mother couldn't afford it. So she wiped her hands carefully, put her wedding ring back on, and said no . . .

1. **Choose a situation and improvise** it together, perhaps with one group improvising in front of the whole class.

2. **While you are improvising**, take your time; do not worry about how the scene will end; and do not be afraid to stop and talk about what you are doing, exchange ideas, and even to start again.

3. **Playwriting**
   Later, write your own version of the drama as a short scripted play. Or write a version of the drama about the son missing from home. Or write a play based on any other idea of your own.

4. **Perhaps write the drama in the form of notes** for the different characters (as with the structured improvisation on the missing son). If so, remember to divide your notes into: a) instructions for everyone; and b) separate instructions for each character, and remember to give every character some kind of motive that will create conflict with other characters.

Later, read each other's plays and if possible, improvise any structured improvisations that have been written.

Discuss the plays – did each character have a definite intention? Was there any conflict? Was there any dramatic irony?

12 Food and Health

This Unit consists of a set of articles of different kinds concerned with the relationship between eating and health.

Working in pairs or small groups, read them through. Talk about them as you read them.

Make a note of any difficult or unusual words; talk about them; work out what they probably mean from the ways they are used. Later, check their meanings in a dictionary.

When you have finished reading and talking about the articles, answer the questions on them at the end of the Unit.

Item 1

Prevention and health: everybody's business

A century ago only six babies out of ten lived to become adults. They died young because of lack of food, bad living conditions and ignorance. In the 1870s, a British boy could expect to live until he was 41. A British girl could expect to live till she was 45.

Today this picture has been greatly changed. Most people can expect to live longer than they did in the past. But, sadly, many people still die sooner than they should. Also many people spend years of their lives in poor health which they could have avoided. Think of people suffering from smokers' cough. Or think of old people who cannot move about because their feet are deformed. Think of all the health problems caused by eating too much and by taking too little exercise.

We all need to be more aware of how we can help ourselves and our families to avoid illness.

from an HMSO publication (adapted)

Salt: deadliest spice of all

For decades a scientific minority has argued that a high salt intake is the commonest cause of high blood pressure. A study in Liverpool now seems to have confirmed the relationship.

by Colin Trudge

High blood pressure (also known as hypertension) is a dangerous medical condition. It can cause a stroke, in which a blood vessel bursts in the brain. And it can cause serious heart disease. (It is worth adding that smoking also can cause heart disease.) It now seems that salt is a major cause of high blood pressure. If you stop eating salt, you reduce the chance of having high blood pressure. This is the main point made in a recent study in Liverpool.

There have been other studies of the effects of salt. One of the best known was by an American, Lewis K. Dahl, who studied the effects of salt on rats. He studied 32,000 of them. And though rats are rats and humans are humans, his findings are important.

The blood pressure of rats normally stays the same throughout their lives. So too does that of all other animals in the wild (as far as is known) and that of some groups of human beings. Only in some human societies (like ours) does blood pressure tend to rise with age. But Dahl found he could induce the blood pressure of rats to rise by various methods, and that the method that worked most efficiently was to add sodium (as salt) to their diets.

The rats' response, however, was far from simple, and far from uniform. There was always a delay, a latent period, before the rats responded. The response was not related simply to dose. Also different individuals responded to different degrees (Figure1). Some unfortunates became extremely hypertensive within a couple of months on a high salt diet, and then died. Some pursued a similarly fatal route, but took a year or more. In some, blood pressure rose quickly – though after a delay – to a new high level, and then remained steady. Some animals, about 20 per cent, did not respond at all.

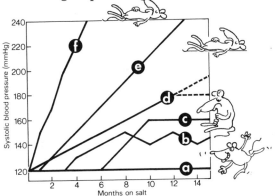

Fig 1   *On a high salt diet, some rats died quickly from high blood pressure; others responded less dramatically; and others did not respond at all. What of humans?*

from the *New Scientist*, 4 June 1981 (adapted)

Item 3

REPRINTED FROM THE BRITISH EDITION OF *READER'S DIGEST*

How to Avoid a Heart Attack

Heart disease is Britain's biggest single killer. Before the age of 65, one man in five is struck down by a heart attack. Women, although less at risk especially until the menopause, are also vulnerable. Between 35 and 65, their death toll is around 8000 a year against 29,000 for male victims in the same age group. Yet many of these deaths could have been avoided, argues Dr Keith Ball, chairman of the Coronary Prevention Group, in this Reader's Digest interview.

Q: Dr Ball, is there any way of knowing that one's life is at risk?

Yes. If anyone in your family had a stroke or heart attack before the age of 60, there is certainly a greater than average chance that you will have one. But for the rest of us the way we live reveals the main dangers, and these can be readily identified. One of the greatest hazards is due to our over-rich diet.

Consider what many of us most enjoy eating – bacon and egg breakfasts, sausages and chips, hamburgers, the crackling on roast pork, butter melting on under-done steaks, dollops of fresh cream on apple tart with a crust made with butter or lard. And there are those full fat cheeses – Stilton, Cheddar or Gruyère. Our high-fat diet . . . is among the most serious causes of heart attack.

Q: Does this mean that the victims were fatally over-weight?

Many certainly were over-weight. But that was not necessarily the fatal factor: there is danger in the raised level of cholesterol in the blood.

Cholesterol is a waxy, yellow-white substance produced mostly in the liver and essential to our survival. We need it to insulate our nerves and to make cell membranes and hormones. But when we have too much of it we can be in trouble. In time, excess cholesterol can clog the arteries – a condition known as atherosclerosis – and so dangerously reduce the blood supply to the brain or heart. When this happens, the victim suffers a stroke or a heart attack.

Q: Is there any way to avoid producing too much cholesterol?

Yes. Possibly nearly a third of the supply is produced not in the liver but from our high-fat diet. This is more than we need and when it is reduced the benefits can be striking. A ten year study in America involving nearly 4000 men, all of whom had high blood cholesterol levels, convincingly made the case. Half of them were given a drug that reduces cholesterol in the body, the other half a placebo. The results . . .

showed that those taking the drug had about one-twelfth less cholesterol in their blood than the others. They suffered 19 per cent fewer non-fatal heart attacks than the others, and their cardiac death rate was 24 per cent lower.

Q: So by changing diet you could cut the risk of a heart attack?

Most certainly – but this will be much less effective if you happen to be a heavy smoker. Smoking is a crucial cause of heart attacks especially in men and women below 50 – indeed it is unusual to find such a patient who doesn't smoke. Particularly at risk are women over 35 who are on the contraceptive pill and smoke.

Q: How does smoking affect the heart?

Nicotine stimulates pro-duction of adrenaline and makes the heart beat harder and faster. Carbon monoxide in cigarette smoke combines with haemoglobin and reduces the amount of oxygen available to help the heart make the necessary extra effort. In addition, nicotine and carbon monoxide both encourage thrombosis – or clotting – in the coronary arteries. It is like putting your foot on the accelerator while using low-grade petrol and pinching the fuel pipe at the same time. No wonder the heart doesn't like it.

Q: How do you know if you have high blood pressure?
You don't. Only a check by your doctor will show if your blood pressure is raised beyond a safe level. It is best to have such a check once every five years, then safeguards can be taken if necessary. When pressure is only moderately raised it can often be controlled by weight reduction, by halving the amount of salt consumed and having no more than two alcoholic drinks a day.

Q: How do salt and alcohol affect blood pressure?
The processes are uncertain. What we do know is that in some communities where much salt is eaten, as in parts of Japan, high rates of blood pressure and stroke occur. Alcoholics also tend to have higher blood pressures which drop when they abstain.

Q: What is the surest way to prevent a heart attack?
Adopt a healthier diet. Stop smoking. Take regular exercise. The right diet is one that is lower in saturated fats which normally come from dairy products, meat fat and most cakes and pastries. Instead of fatty meats, eat more poultry and fish. Soft margarine high in polyunsaturates is better than butter. But if you use butter, spread it thinly. If you don't like skimmed milk, use semi-skimmed. Cut down on sugar.
Eat plenty of fruit and vegetables and don't forget that pulses are high in protein and can make tasty dishes. Get used to the taste of wholemeal bread instead of sliced white.
The best form of exercise is the one you really enjoy. Cycling, swimming or jogging are all suitable. To be effective, exercise should be strenuous enough to leave you short of breath and to raise your pulse rate. But it should be started slowly and steadily increased. For those fit enough – by far the majority – a useful guide is 20 minutes' vigorous exercise three times a week. But if you are in doubt, consult your doctor.
In addition to helping you to control your weight, physical training gives the heart muscle greater reserve. Physical exertion helps to keep the coronary arteries open.

Q: Is there proof that such preventive measures are effective?
There is very strong evidence. In Australia, where changes in diet have taken place – a decrease in the consumption of meat, milk, cheese and butter, and an increase in the consumption of margarine high in polyunsaturates – the coronary death rate has fallen by about 20 per cent.
In the United States, the improvement is even more striking. There, in less than 20 years, consumption of eggs dropped by 12 per cent, butter by 24 per cent, animal fats and oils by 39 per cent, while fish consumption increased by more than a fifth, that of vegetable fats and oils by well over half.
At the same time, more American adults were taking up some kind of physical exercise or sport. Twenty years ago fewer than a quarter of them went in for such activities; today three-quarters do so – nearly half of them on a daily basis.
And in the United States the coronary mortality rate has dropped by more than 30 per cent.

Q: At what age should we start taking preventive measures?
Undoubtedly in childhood. That is when faulty eating habits start. Young children soon develop a taste for sugary, fatty foods which is often reinforced by school dinners. Children in primary schools often try their first cigarettes and become smokers. The result is that, by the teens and twenties, damage to the arteries may already appear in those who are otherwise quite well.
So childhood is the best time to develop healthy heart habits. But whatever your age the time to act is now if you are to avoid the horror of a time bomb going off in your chest.

from the *Reader's Digest*, 1984; ©1984, the Reader's Digest

Item 4

Food and Crime

There is now a lot of evidence that shows there is some connection between food and crime. In other words, what we eat may cause us to become criminals. This seems to be true of both children and adults.

For example, a lack of iron in the body can cause children to behave badly at home and school. When they are given extra supplies of iron in their diet, their behaviour improves.

One study has shown that many criminals live most of their lives on a diet that is poor in vitamins, and especially in Vitamin B1 (thiamine). They tend to like food that is high in calories but low in good food value. Many of them have also drunk a lot of alcohol and many of them have used drugs. All these habits upset the chemistry of the body and make it hard for people to control their own behaviour.

It is too soon to say that we now know for certain that there is a strong link between eating and crime. But there seems no doubt that there is a link.

from *Eating Habits* by Rïse Phender

Item 5

Ten Ways to Better Eating and Better Health

1. Avoid dairy products, especially butter and eggs.
2. Avoid fried foods, especially bacon and egg, sausages, and fish and chips.
3. If you need to fry your food, do not use lard. Use oils that are highly unsaturated. These are corn, soya, sunflower and safflower oils. These can be bought very cheaply in most chemists'.
4. Reduce the amount of meat you eat. Especially reduce the amount of red meat (such as beef) and pork, and any meat that is fatty.
5. Cut out sugar. Cut down on sweets and on sweet foods.
6. Cut out salt.
7. Eat plenty of fresh fruit and fresh vegetables and salads, and potatoes baked in their jackets. Eat plenty of carrots.
8. If you cook your vegetables, do not BOIL them. This kills all their goodness. Instead, you should steam them.
9. Always eat a good breakfast. Never go without eating a good breakfast. This is the most important meal of the day and should include a good cereal such as shredded wheat sprinkled with natural bran and wheatgerm. This will give you some of the roughage that your body needs. To this you can add fruit juice and any fruit that is available.
10. Cut down on coffee. It increases the cholesterol in the blood. One cup a day is a maximum.

from *Better Eating, Better Health* by Celia Mirren

Who's a Pig?

by Alan Long

The average Western man eats his way through one cow, seven bullocks, 36 pigs, 36 sheep and 550 poultry in his lifetime. If instead people ate the equivalent of the tonnes of plant food necessary to sustain these animals, it would not only feed five times as many, but keep them in better health.

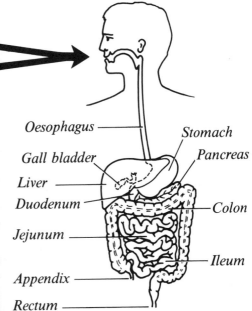

Oesophagus

Stomach

Pancreas

Gall bladder

Liver

Duodenum

Colon

Jejunum

Ileum

Appendix

Rectum

from the *New Scientist*, 5 February 1981

Item 7

Educating people to eat well

I make no apology for saying that the health of the majority of human beings depends more on their nutrition than it does on any other single factor. However important and dramatic have been the advances in hygiene, medicine and surgery, it is still true that even more important would be the effects that proper nutrition would have on human sickness and mortality. For this reason, I believe that the ultimate objective of nutritionists must be the nutrition education of the public.

The need for nutrition education of the public implies that people are eating less well than they could be eating, and that they can be persuaded to eat better through nutrition education ... However, it is now realised that knowledge does not necessarily determine behaviour. What we know is not necessarily what we do. London housewives knew, or thought they knew, that brown bread was nutritionally better than white, and that the major cause of dental decay was the eating of sweets. Yet nine out of ten ate white bread, and most of them bought sweets in large quantities for their children.

Another example is the work done by educators in Peruvian villages some 30 years ago. In the classical manner, the villagers were told about calories, protein, vitamins and mineral elements, and how important it was to eat the right foods to ensure that they got all these items. A year later, the nutritionists found the villagers eating precisely as they had done before. They had however changed their classification of food so that what they still considered good foods were now called vitamin A, the next best foods were called vitamin B, and so along the alphabet.

In order to get people to change their eating habits, it is not necessary to describe the vitamins in terms of the detailed signs and symptoms of scurvy, or beri-beri ... It would be better for people to eat a correct diet for quite the wrong reasons – for example, because they believed it would help them to converse with the little green men whom they expected to land in their garden – than to eat the wrong diet even though they could recite the properties of all the vitamins and mineral elements.

The object of nutrition education is to change dietary behaviour.

adapted from *Objectives and Methods in Nutrition Education – Let's Start Again*
(Lecture given to the *Society for Nutrition Education* in Montreal, July 1980)

John Yudkin, MA, MD, PhD, FRCP, FRIC, FIBiol
Emeritus Professor of Nutrition, Queen Elizabeth College, London University

Item 8

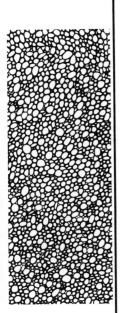

Survey of Students' Eating Habits

	1st Class YES	1st Class NO	2nd Class YES	2nd Class NO	3rd Class YES	3rd Class NO
Generally eat good breakfast	16	8	12	12	20	4
Avoid salt	1	23	4	20	1	23
Avoid sugar and sweets	4	20	8	16	4	20
Often eat fresh fruit	7	17	8	16	14	10
Often eat fresh vegetables	4	20	12	12	14	10
Avoid red meats	0	24	1	23	2	22
Eat brown bread	4	20	6	18	10	14
Avoid processed foods	0	24	7	17	10	14
Avoid coffee	1	23	6	18	4	20
Avoid fried foods	1	23	2	22	4	20

This is an extract from a students' survey of their eating habits in three different classes of 17- and 18-year-old students.

Each class had 24 students.

N.B. When the first question ('Do you eat a good breakfast?') was rephrased as, 'Do you eat a good breakfast, without fried foods?' the answers changed slightly, as follows:

> 1st class: 12 Yes, 12 No.
> 2nd class: 10 Yes, 14 No.
> 3rd class: 17 Yes,   7 No.

125

QUESTIONS on all the items

Discuss the questions in your groups, but write down your own individual answers.

For Questions 1 to 10, you have to check which of the items confirms (or confirm) the statement that is made. For example, if Item 6 gives you the information that is in Question 1, you would just write down 'Item 6'. In some cases, there may be more than one item that gives you the information.

Which item (or items) tell(s) you each of the following?

1 Children born today in Britain can be expected to live longer than children born a century or so ago.
2 Most people eat a large number of pigs, bullocks, sheep and poultry.
3 People in Japan tend to suffer from high blood pressure.
4 People's blood pressure tends to go up and down.
5 The blood pressure of rats tends to stay the same throughout their lives.

6 What we eat may cause us to become criminals.
7 Coffee can be dangerous.
8 People often continue to eat bad foods even after they learn they are bad for them.
9 Many students have bad eating habits.
10 Education has not done much to improve students' eating habits.

Which of these statements is true according to the items in this Unit? Just write down
TRUE *or* FALSE, *and give the number(s) of the item (or items) that give you your answer.*

11 Very few students eat a good breakfast.
12 We should try to change people's eating habits.
13 Vegetables should be boiled, not steamed.
14 Vegetables should be steamed, not boiled.
15 We should cut down on sugar.
16 Changing your diet will not reduce your chance of having a heart attack.

17 Alcohol can cause high blood pressure.
18 We should eat wholemeal bread.
19 Since Americans have increased the amount of exercise they do every day, and reduced their eating of bad foods, their health has improved.
20 Animal fats are dangerous. Vegetable fats are much less dangerous.

_____ PREPARING A TALK _____

Choose a topic of your own. Perhaps choose one that is related to another aspect of health – or fitness – or any personal interest of yours.

Collect a small set of materials to illustrate your topic and to help you to plan and make notes for a talk you could give to other members of your class. Perhaps invite your listeners to look at some of the materials before or during your talk.

13 Images

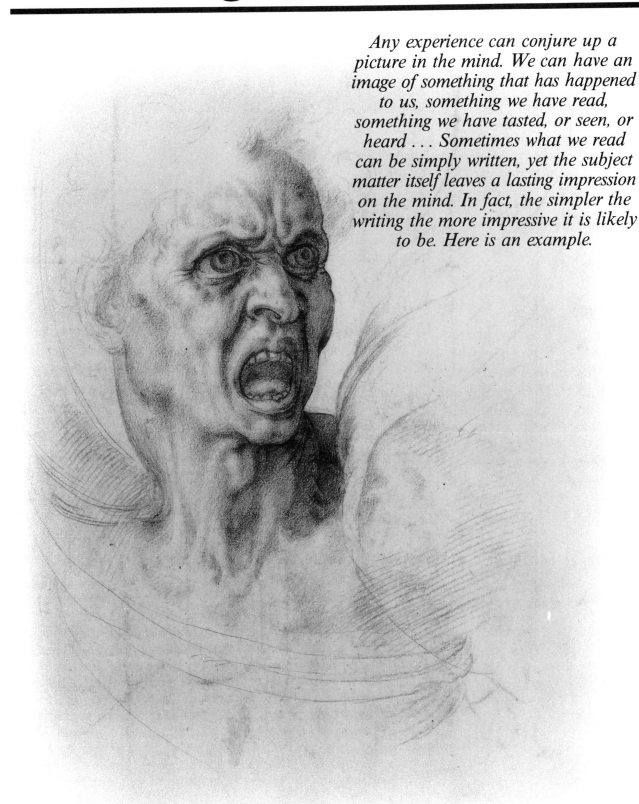

Any experience can conjure up a picture in the mind. We can have an image of something that has happened to us, something we have read, something we have tasted, or seen, or heard ... Sometimes what we read can be simply written, yet the subject matter itself leaves a lasting impression on the mind. In fact, the simpler the writing the more impressive it is likely to be. Here is an example.

Head of a Lost Soul *by Michelangelo (1475–1564)*

Punishment at Sea

John Wetherell was pressed into service in the British Navy at about the time of the Napoleonic Wars.

Here he describes the punishment of a 17-year-old boy who, like himself, had been forced to serve in the navy, and who tried to escape.

All hands were called once more. The Marines all placed on the gangways and front of the quarter deck all under arms to protect the Bloodthirsty monster [the captain] in his barbarous tortures. Old Douse-the-Glim [Master-at-Arms] presented himself to the quarter deck, reporting the prisoner ready.

'Seize him up,' answered the son of thunder, 'and as for you Boatswains Mates do your duty or I will see your back bones.'

'Oh Captain for the sake of my poor Mother have Mercy on me and forgive me.'

'No Sir, if I forgive you I hope God will never forgive me. Go on Boatswains Mate.'

'Master at Arms how many has he had?'

'One dozen and five Sir.'

'Go on Bosun's Mate.' He faints.

'Stop,' says the doctor.

'No, Sir, he is only acting. Go on I say.'

He lay as still as any dead man. Poor fellow, that was the time ev'ry heart not made of stone whisper'd revenge. We had to grin and bear it.

By this time he had received two dozen, another Bosun's Mate had orders to go on – not any signs of life was to be seen in him. The Doctor felt his pulse and ordered him not to have any more lashes at present, he being entirely insensible of what was transacting.

'Well Sir,' says Wilkinson [the captain] 'Your orders shall be obey'd in that respect, but mine shall in another. Mr Hill, [the Master-at-Arms] take that fellow forward, and you Boatswain's Mates make him fast with a rope and heave him overboard. I know how to bring him to his senses again.'

Accordingly his orders were obeyed. They hove him three times overboard and then hove him on the deck, not any signs of life in him. Doctor Graham order'd him below and to be wrapped up in a blanket. In the course of an hour they had let blood from him, he began to groan, and afterwards cry out for his Mother.

[*The same writer also describes another punishment for a different offender.*]

'Old Andrew McCarthy can not be forgot by me he was aged and made cooks mate. Drinking a little ships beer . . . rather freely after his work was done some enemy reported him to the quarter deck. He was taken aft put in *irons* all night to ruminate on his past frolic. At daylight next morning this unfortunate mortal was called on deck and order'd to be lash'd up in the forerigging and salt water to be poured down his throat thro' the help of a funnel, which was done and repeated several times, until the water passed through him as clear as when administered. He was then left in the rigging the way they termed *a spread Eagle*. This proved to be one of those cold sleety mornings quite frequent in the North Sea. After remaining in this horrid situation nearly two hours orders came to cut him down and make him scrub the *coppers* ev'ry morning for one month.

reprinted in *Nelson's Navy* by Patrick Richardson

But life at sea was not always so grim, as this episode shows. It is from a journal written slightly earlier, in the second half of the eighteenth century.

Cat Overboard! ————————————————————

A most tragical Incident fell out this day at Sea. While the Ship was under Sail, but making, as will appear, no great Way, a Kitten, one of four of the Feline Inhabitants of the Cabin, fell from the Window into the Water; Alarm was immediately given to the Captain, who was then upon Deck, and received it with the utmost Concern. He immediately gave Orders to the Steersman. The Sails were instantly slackened, and all Hands employed to recover the poor Animal. I was, I own, extremely surprised at all this, for, if Puss had had nine thousand, instead of nine Lives, I concluded they had been all lost. The Boatswain, however, having stript himself of his Jacket, Breeches and Shirt, he leapt boldly into the Water, and, to my great Astonishment, in a few Minutes, returned to the Ship, bearing the motionless Animal in his Mouth. The Kitten was now exposed to Air and Sun on the Deck, where its Life, of which it retained no Symptoms, was despaired by all.

Having felt his Loss like a Man, the Captain resolved to shew he could bear it like one; and having declared, he had rather have lost a Cask of Rum or Brandy, betook himself to threshing at Backgammon with the *Portuguese* Friar, in which innocent Amusement they passed their leisure hours.

But as I have, perhaps, a little too wantonly endeavoured to raise the tender Passions of my Readers, in this Narrative, I should think myself unpardonable if I concluded it, without giving them the Satisfaction of hearing that the Kitten at last recovered, to the great Joy of the good Captain.

from *Journal of a Voyage to Lisbon* by **Henry Fielding (abridged)**

For Discussion

1 When you think back to the first passage, what image comes most powerfully to your mind?

2 Now look again at the passage and consider which words and phrases are most effective in creating that image in your mind.

3 Consider the same questions (1 and 2 above) in connection with the second passage.

4 Spelling and punctuation (including the use of capital letters) change from time to time. Are there any examples of this in these two pieces of writing?

PUNCTUATION: Semicolon

A semicolon (;) can be used instead of a full stop where the writer wishes to show that two different statements (both of which could be sentences) are closely connected with each other.

An example would be: **George went to Sweden for his holiday; Barbara went to Greece.**

Here both the statements make complete sense on their own, but the semicolon is used to show that they both closely relate to each other. In effect, they both say one thing – where they went. Note and discuss the uses of the semicolon in *Cat Overboard!*

Hyphen (-)

The hyphen is used to join words together when they need to be read as one thing. Examples from *Punishment at Sea* are

    'Master-at-Arms' *and* **'Douse-the-Glim'.**

In general, the hyphen is used to make meaning clear to the reader, to avoid any ambiguity or double meaning.

For example, compare: **He wore a deep-red velvet cloak.**
                            (*meaning the velvet cloak was deep-red*)

      and   **He wore a deep, red, velvet cloak.**
                            (*meaning the velvet cloak was deep and red*)

What would the following
sentence mean without
the hyphens?   **He was a tight-fisted ugly-looking fellow.**

Dash (–)

The dash is used to separate words, while the hyphen is used to join them together.

Generally the dash is used to mark off some kind of sharp break or interruption in a sentence.

For example: **You mustn't do that – I said, you mustn't!**

Find another example in the first extract, *Punishment at Sea.*

Sometimes two dashes are used to show the beginning and the end of an interruption in the middle of a sentence.

For example: **If you do that – and I advise you not to – you will have to face the consequences.**

For individual work

Rewrite these sentences with any necessary changes of punctuation. Do not alter the order of the words.

1 The punishment if you can call it that was too severe.

2 The captain clearly enjoyed it the men hated it.

3 The cat of nine tails was used.

4 There was a long silence after the punishment had taken place.

5 The men were deeply angry the officers were worried the victim was nearly dead.

6 The captain shouted, 'Now men you see what you look at me when I'm speaking.'

7 We all expected life to be hard on a man of war.

8 Nobody had ever thought that life would be as bad as this at least not before they met the Captain.

TWO LOVE POEMS

Slow Motion

In the secret dark
Of the morning
I dreamed of you.
Dawn-lit, and favoured by flaming suns.
You wandered through my mind.

One by one the swans
Challenged the sky.
And I flew to join them.
From below you watched me.
Your face up-turned
And pleading.
So I came to rest on the lake.
In slow motion.

Kirsty Seymour-Ure (17)

He Wishes for the Cloths of Heaven

Had I the heavens' embroidered cloths,
Enwrought with golden and silver light,
The blue and the dim and the dark cloths
Of night and light and the half-light,
I would spread the cloths under your feet:
But I, being poor, have only my dreams;
I have spread my dreams under your feet;
Tread softly because you tread on my dreams.

W. B. Yeats

For Discussion

1 What moods do the two poems express?
2 What different images do they create?

Head of a Young Woman *by Leonardo (1452–1519)*

131

From a South African Prison

Cold

the clammy cement
sucks our naked feet

a rheumy yellow bulb
lights a damp grey wall

the stubbled grass
wet with three o'clock dew
is black with glittery edges;

we sit on the concrete,
stuff with our fingers
the sugarless pap
into our mouths

then labour erect;

form lines;

steel ourselves into fortitude
or accept an image of ourselves
numb with resigned acceptance;

the grizzled senior warder comments:
"Things like these
I have no time for;

they are worse than rats;
you can only shoot them."

Overhead
the large frosty glitter of the stars
the Southern Cross flowering low;

the chains on our ankles
and wrists
that pair us together
jangle

glitter.

We begin to move
awkwardly.

Young Dancer, Kirov Ballet School

from *Letters to Martha* by Dennis Brutus

The Dancer

Music flows.
He dances gracefully,
As light as a flame,
A motion in his fantasy.
Silent poetry,
The art of all arts,
Dancing is to live,
Emotions in the air,
Leaping,
Rotational movements.
He accelerates,
The melody quickens its pace,
Twisting,
Turning,
He moves freely,
Where his legs take him,
The dance reaches its climax,
Gradually swiftness hesitates,
Deceleration,
Still as graceful,
The music stops,
Sweat on his supple spine,
Position poised.

Rosemary Billington (14)

Grandfather's Holiday

Blue sky, paddy fields, grandchild's play,
Deep ponds, diving-stage, child's holiday;
Tree shade, barn corners, catch-me-if-you-dare,
Undergrowth, *pārul*-bushes, life without care.
Green paddy all a-quiver, hopeful as a child,
Child prancing, river dancing, waves running wild.

Bespectacled grandfather old man am I,
Trapped in my work like a spiderwebbed fly.
Your games are my games, my proxy holiday,
Your laugh the sweetest music I shall ever play.
Your joy is mine, my mischief in your eyes,
Your delight the country where my freedom lies.

Autumn sailing in, now, steered by your play,
Bringing white *śiuli*-flowers to grace your holiday.
Pleasure of the chilly air tingling me at night,
Blown from Himālaya on the breeze of your delight.
Dawn in Āśvin, flower-forcing roseate sun,
Dressed in the colours of a grandchild's fun.

Flooding of my study with your leaps and your capers,
Work gone, books flying, avalanche of papers.
Arms round my neck, in my lap bounce thump –
Hurricane of freedom in my heart as you jump.
Who has taught you, how he does it, I shall never know –
You're the one who teaches me to let myself go.

Rabindranath Tagore
(translated by William Radice)

Man and Dog *by Jean Mohr*

For Discussion

1 Choose one word or short phrase
   from each poem that you think best
   expresses the mood or feeling of
   each.

2 Choose one word or short phrase
   from each poem that most clearly
   creates an image in your mind.

3 Suggest one word or short phrase
   to express the mood or feeling of
   each of the pictures in this section –
   *Head of a Lost Soul, Head of
   Young Woman, Young Dancer, Man
   and Dog* and *Le Salon de l'Artiste*.
   Make a list of all the different words
   or phrases that seem appropriate
   and then choose the best one.

133

Life in a Racing Stable

Thomas Holcroft worked as a stableboy in the late eighteenth century. This is an extract from his memoirs.

All the boys in the stable rise at the same hour, from half-past two in spring, to between four and five in the depth of winter. The horses hear them when they awaken each other, and neigh, to denote their eagerness to be fed. Being dressed, the boy begins with carefully clearing out the manger, and giving a feed of oats, which he is obliged no less carefully to sift. He then proceeds to dress the litter; that is, to shake the bed on which the horse has been lying, remove whatever is wet or unclean, and keep the remaining straw in the stable for another time. The whole stables are then thoroughly swept, the few places for fresh air are kept open, the great heat of the stable gradually cooled, and the horse, having ended his first feed, is roughly cleaned and dressed. In about half an hour after they begin ... the horses have been rubbed down, and reclothed, saddled, each turned in his stall, then bridled, mounted, and the whole string goes out to morning exercise. He that leads is the first: for each boy knows his place.

Except by accident, the race-horse never trots. He must either walk or gallop. And in exercise, even when it is the hardest, the gallop begins slowly and gradually, and increases till the horse is nearly at full speed. When he has galloped half a mile, the boy begins to push him forward, without relaxation, for another half-mile. This is at the period when the horses are in full exercise, to which they come by degrees. The boy that can best regulate these degrees among those of light weight, is generally chosen to lead the gallop. That is, he goes first out of the stable, and first returns ...

The morning's exercise often extends to four hours, and the evening's to much about the same time. Being once in the stable, each lad begins his labour. He leads the horse into his stall, ties him up, rubs down his legs with straw, and takes off his saddle and body clothes. He curries him carefully with both currycomb and brush, and never leaves him till he has thoroughly cleaned his skin, so that neither spot nor wet, nor any appearance of neglect may be seen about him. The horse is then reclothed, and suffered to repose for some time ... All this is performed, and the stables are once more shut up, about nine o'clock.

Accustomed to this life, the boys are very little overcome by fatigue, except that early in the morning they may be drowsy. I have sometimes fallen slightly asleep at the beginning of the first brushing gallop. But if they are not weary, they are hungry, and they make themselves ample amends for all they have done. Nothing perhaps can exceed the enjoyment of a stableboy's breakfast. What then may not be said of mine, who had so long been used to suffer hunger, and so seldom found the means of satisfying it? Our breakfast consisted of new milk, or milk porridge, then the cold meat of the preceding day, most exquisite Gloucester cheese, fine white bread, and concluded with plentiful draughts of table beer. All this did not overload the stomach, or in the least deprive me of my youthful activity, except that like others I might sometimes take a nap for an hour, after so small a portion of sleep.

For my own part, so total and striking was the change which had taken place in my situation, that I could not but feel it very sensibly. I was more conscious of it than most boys would have been, and therefore not a little satisfied. The former part of my life had most of it been spent in turmoil, and often in singular wretchedness ... I had been exposed to every want, every weariness. Happy had been the meal where I had enough. Rich to me was the rag that kept me warm. And heavenly the pillow, no matter what, or how hard, on which I could lay my head to sleep.

from *The Memoirs of Thomas Holcroft, 1745–1809*

Group Discussion

1 Make a note of any difficult or unusual words. Talk about what they probably mean and then check their meanings in a dictionary.

2 Which of these would be the best subheading for the first paragraph?

A Bright Start   First Jobs   Horses and Stableboys

Choose the subheading that most clearly summarises what the whole paragraph is about.

3 Devise a suitable subheading for each of the other paragraphs.

4 What are the three or four main things that the passage tells you about life and work in the eighteenth century?

5 What are the three or four main things that the passage tells you about Thomas Holcroft?

Later, compare your answers with the rest of the class.

Le Salon de l'Artiste, Rue la Boétie *by Pablo Picasso*

Three Projects

All these three projects involve the use of a library where you can browse and investigate.

1 Photographs

Browse through collections of photographs, such as:

a) photographs of different places and of places at various times in the past. There are many anthologies of places in Britain, for instance, in the Edwardian era, or in Victorian times.

b) photographs by distinguished photographers such as Bert Hardy, André Kertesz, Cecil Beaton and E. O. Hoppé.

Choose half a dozen of the most interesting photographs and after noting their titles, the names of the photographers and the books in which you have found them, write a short collection of words and phrases to describe each one.

2 Paintings

Browse through collections of books showing the work of different painters, such as Rembrandt, Picasso, Van Gogh, Hockney. Then, as with Project 1, choose half a dozen of the most interesting ones, and devise a collection of words and phrases to describe each one.

In both cases, do not write sentences, but choose language that seems to you to create the picture you are describing.

3 Poems

Browse through some anthologies, such as _The Rattle Bag_ (edited by Seamus Heaney and Ted Hughes), _The Penguin Book of Modern African Poetry_ (edited by Gerald Moore and Ullie Beier), and _News for Babylon_ (edited by James Berry). Choose half a dozen poems by different poets that seem to you to create powerful images in the reader's mind.

Later use any of the ideas you have got from any of these projects as a basis for writing some poems of your own.

14 Working Lives

Talking to Parents

A group of students interviewed their parents about their own early experiences of work and their advice to young people today. Here are some of their reports, either as transcripts *or as* summaries.

Mr Barrett

Q How did it feel when you first started work?

A Initially I felt excited about leaving school and working. My education was very sparse and limited. My first job was in a corn merchants. I didn't like it very much. I soon realised there was no future in this job and packed it in. There was a lot of opportunity for errand boy jobs, but worthwhile jobs, jobs with a future, were very rare and hard to come by.

Q Are you still doing the same job?

A No. Soon after the merchants' job I was lucky and managed to get a job as a boiler-coverer, covering heated materials. Then shortly after that, War intervened and I joined the army. I liked the army, obviously not the war. But I found the army catered for the adventurous side of me. After the war, I got married and then joined Fords Motor Company as a tool setter.

Q What were conditions like at Fords?

A Now, I think, they are the best ever. The Unions see to that. There are also plenty of facilities.

Q Can conditions be improved?

A I would say everything can be improved. Nothing is perfect. It's a shame that a lot of people take advantage of conditions, especially with the backing of the unions.

Q If you could afford it, would you rather not work?

A No, I don't think I could. If I had money I'd run a small business but I could never do nothing. I'm not a lazy person.

Q What work would you prefer?

A I don't know. If I could have a job where I could enjoy it, and then the wage packet at the end of the week is a bonus – then I'd be a very happy man. The reason I work is to support my family.

Q Do you think most people enjoy their work?

A In most cases I'd say no. As it is, I am relatively happy about my work, but I'd say only the minority enjoy their work. My definition of work is to bring home money so that me and my family can enjoy ourselves in our free time.

Q What kind of advice would you give young people about to start work?

A Well, I'd like to see you in a position where you can pick and choose the job you want. To do this it means working hard and getting exam passes. To all young people, I'd say, work hard at school and college so you get a job you want rather than being forced into a job you don't want to do. Remember a job should last you a lifetime.

Mrs Hemmings

'... When I was your age, most girls did not think seriously about finding a good job and having a career. Now they have to. Everything has changed in three very important ways: first, there's a lot of unemployment; secondly, girls must be able to make their own way in the world; third, you must be willing to move around. It's no good a girl thinking she can make her life and her work down the street from her own mother. I hope that's what they're teaching girls about today in schools and colleges: the world is a different place especially for girls!'

Mrs Granger

She said that times have changed. When she left school it was quite easy to get a job, but now of course it's different. She said her advice to anyone leaving school or college is to get as many qualifications as possible so one can go for a fairly wide field of jobs. She said that one has to remember that one is not just competing with students in one's own area but with students from all over the country.

Mr Beech

... Now 21 years on, Tom is still a lorry driver, though now self-employed. Asked why he never expanded, he replies that he couldn't be bothered to employ others, even if it meant more wealth. If he didn't have to work and could afford not to, Tom says that he would work only when he felt like it. If he could do this, he would be a used commercial vehicle dealer and renovator of commercials in his spare time.

His advice to young job hunters is to get a good and varied education whilst you can, so you are not tied down to one thing.

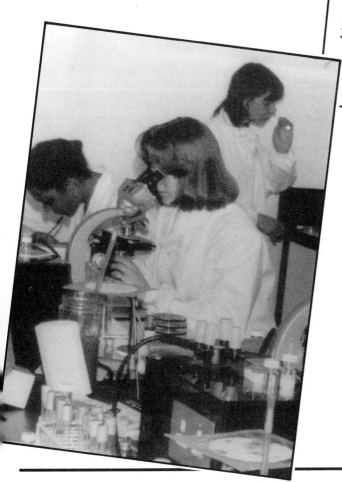

For Discussion

1 Mr Barrett says that most people do not enjoy their work. Do you think this is true?

2 In what different ways do these parents think that times have changed since they started working?

3 On what point do all four of these parents agree?

4 Both Mr Barrett and Mr Beech think they would work even if they could afford not to. Do you think this is true of most people?

5 Mrs Hemmings says that girls must now be prepared to move around to find work. Why does she think this? Is this also true of boys?

Students Talking to Students

The same group of students who had interviewed their parents also interviewed each other, chatting about their attitudes to their own futures, their hopes and fears. Here is the report written by one of the students.

All of us are fascinated and baffled by the future, especially our own future. Many of us read the horoscope in the newspaper not because we really believe what it tells us, but because you never know, the horoscope may turn out to be true! Wrong prediction may be better than no prediction at all!

When we talked in class about our futures, it was soon obvious that most of us have fantasies: we have marvellous dreams for ourselves that are not very likely to come true. Some people may think these fantasies are bad and foolish. But I don't. I think it's a good thing to fantasise about what the future holds for you, it gives you something to live for. It may sound corny, but where there's hope there's life!

These are some of the fantasies that our group talked about. One wants to be a professional soccer-player; one wants to be rich enough to retire at 40 and buy a body-building centre; one wants to be a hairdresser or beautician in a TV studio working with the famous stars; one wants to get rich quickly so that he can drive back to school in a pink Porsche and say hello to all the teachers who told him he was thick.

Everybody, even those with great fantasies, also had more down-to-earth ideas. These include: working in dad's garage; getting a job at the Co-op; joining the police force; training as a computer operator; becoming a secretary; training as a nursery nurse; and becoming a fireman.

Of course, nowadays even down-to-earth jobs are hard to get. So in a way, even any ambition may be something of a fantasy. But there is no way one can plan for the future without also planning for some kind of job. After all, the entire class want to earn enough money to marry and raise a family, apart from two students in the group who said they did not think they wanted to get married ever. Everybody else said they hoped to marry before they are 30, and most said they wanted to marry before they are 25.

Also, most but not all of the students would like to travel and see something of the world, but later they would like to live fairly near to their parents. They also (most of them) hope to earn enough money to be able to help their parents when they grow old.

So as you can see, in our class hope springs eternal. We live in a world of high unemployment and nuclear defence. Any minute of any day we could all be blown sky high (or higher) on our way to the dole queue, but that doesn't seem to stop us having our dreams!

Paul Tufnell

For Class Discussion

1   What is a fantasy?
2   Why does Paul Tufnell think that 'any ambition' nowadays may be 'something of a fantasy'?
3   Do you read your horoscope? Do you agree with Paul Tufnell's claim that 'wrong prediction may be better than no prediction at all'?

For Group Discussion

Talk about and make a short report on these questions:
1   What kind of job would you ideally like to have?
2   What would you have to do to stand a chance of getting it?
3   What other hopes do you have for the future?
4   What jobs would you like to have even though they may not be your idea of an ideal job?

Later, report on your discussions to the rest of the class and compare your ideas.

Young Workers Talking

Lesley Brew is a chippy (carpenter). She is working through an apprenticeship with Southwark Council. The council has 80 apprentices in skilled manual trades, Lesley is the only woman.

What made you take up carpentry and joinery?

I was unemployed after working in a youth club for a year and a friend of mine was working on a Job Creation Project doing carpentry. I heard him talking about his work, it sounded interesting and I went to work with him to have a look round. It reminded me of how much I enjoyed messing around with wood when I was a child. I was eventually employed on the project as a trainee carpenter and joiner.

How did you get an apprenticeship?

My basic idea was to work with wood and I wanted a training so I applied to Southwark to do an apprenticeship. The man who interviewed me admitted that he hadn't met many women who wanted to do this kind of work and he asked me if I thought I could cope physically! He pointed out that I would be working outside in the rain and mud. But really this was all said in a straightforward way and I accepted it.

Why do you think girls don't normally go in for this type of work?

Most girls' Mums and Dads don't think it's the right thing. Manual trades are not thought of as being very ladylike. They are expected to be clean and feminine. Most kids are brainwashed at home, at school and by friends. There is always a pressure against this sort of work.

Another thing is that girls and women are not thought of as being responsible, and skilled manual work does mean being able to take responsibility. For instance, if you were a plumber and you didn't seal the pipes properly, well the whole place would be flooded. Careers teachers are not usually known for encouraging women to go in for manual trades.

Do you feel that women are discriminated against at work?

Yes, but one very positive thing about working in the manual trades is that the wages are high. I've heard a lot about women who are discriminated against when they apply for T.O.P.s courses. 'Not tall enough', 'Not experienced enough'. The thing is they don't have any statutory entry requirements so it's up to the individual that interviews you to put you onto a course. I think that if that happens, women should try other Job Centres until they get someone more sympathetic. But then of course, T.O.P.s courses don't run creches and the thought of one on a site . . . well!

What did your friends and family think?

Well, my family thought that it was probably a phase and that I'd drop it in six months.

Some of the men I know did try to dissuade me from doing the training, they thought it was just a hobby. Now that I'm working as a chippy on site they know that it's a job.

What sort of work do you do?

I work on a site off the Walworth Road, converting old properties into council flats. The labourers prepare the place for the chippies. We go in and do the first fixing, the structural work, repairing the roof, timbers, joists and door linings. The plasterers come in and then we do the second fixing; the finer work such as hanging doors, putting in window frames etc.

How do you see the future?

I can see myself as a chippie on a building site, but some women prefer to be self-employed. If you work by yourself it's easier if you have a family, your time can be more flexible and there's no boss. Other women are beginning to work in co-operatives which means they can set up their own nurseries . . .

from *I Want to Write it Down – Writings by Women in Peckham*

For Discussion

1 What different things make a carpenter's work interesting to Lesley Brew?

2 What personal qualities does she seem to have?

3 What is a co-operative?

4 Lesley talks of there being a pressure against girls going in for manual work. Is there any kind of pressure that stops you from even considering certain kinds of work?

Interviews

Polly Toynbee spent time studying the work of interviewers in a Youth Employment Bureau in south Yorkshire. Here are her accounts of two of the interviews.

Both the candidates are 17.

Michael

Michael: 'I'm not getting anywhere, you see. I want to get on in life. I want a job with a future. All these jobs I've had, they won't let me get on. It's no good having jobs that get you no-where all the time.'

Interviewer: 'Well, Michael, tell me what you've been doing since you left school.'

Michael: 'I'm working at a big supermarket you see. They call it Provisions Assistant, but it isn't the job it sounds. I'm stacking dog biscuits and soap packets all day onto the counters. There's no promotion, no training. I tell them I want a chance to get on and they don't do anything about it. I thought Provisions Assistant would mean something to do with buying but it's just stacking.'

Interviewer: 'What did you do before that?'

Michael: 'When I left school? I went to work with my Dad. He has a small firm. I was rewinding transformers. But my brother was there, and we didn't get on. He shouted at me all the time. I left, and my father doesn't want to know any more. My brother doesn't work there now. I might have done some good if I'd stayed, but my Dad doesn't want to know.'

Interviewer: 'Have you had any other jobs, Michael?'

Michael: 'I worked in a bakery.'

Interviewer: 'Why did you leave?'

Michael: 'It was boring work, and no prospects. After that I went as a van assistant in a laundry helping deliveries, but I had an accident in it, and I broke an arm and a leg and I was off work for six months.'

Interviewer: 'I see. Now tell me, you haven't been to a Youth Employment office before?'

Michael: 'No. When I was leaving school I was dead set on working with my Dad, so I didn't need a job. I found the other jobs myself.'

Interviewer: 'What do your parents think you should do? Have you talked to them about it?'

Michael: 'Well, I don't know. I don't think my Dad's bothered. My Mum thinks I should get a good job and get on.'

Interviewer: 'So what sort of job would you like now, Michael?'

Michael: 'Something in the grocery trade. I want to get on to the buying side.'

Interviewer: 'I see. Now just let me look at your file a moment, just so that I can keep it up to date with everything you've done since you left school.'

Michael: 'You see, they say other industries are important, but when it comes to it, food is the only thing everyone has to have. That's why I'm interested in it.'

Interviewer: 'Have you always been keen on a job before you actually do it?'

Michael: 'Yes, I suppose I get disillusioned.'

Interviewer: 'All right, fair enough. Now would you mind if we just go back to your school for a moment? What subjects did you like?'

Michael: 'History. English too.'

Interviewer: 'Why history?'

Michael: 'Um, well it's interesting. You've got to know what went on.'

Interviewer: 'Well, Michael, I think you're right to want a change of job. That super-market chain do tend to work young people into the ground. They're not very good employers. I think the answer for you would be to work in the Co-op. There's one just near where you live. They're nice people and I think you'd have a better time there. They'd give you a day release course too, which is always a good thing.'

Michael: 'Would they let me get on?'

Interviewer: 'They're very good employers.'

An interview with the Co-op was arranged over the telephone.

143

Jean

Interviewer: 'Hello, Jean, I don't think we've met before. But I've got your papers here, if you'll excuse me while I just cast an eye over them? Ah, yes, Jean. Now you were a junior clerk with that finance company. What can I do for you?'

Jean: 'Well, you see, I've always wanted to be a telephonist. When I left school there weren't any jobs and I wondered if you had any now?'

Interviewer: 'That may not be too easy, but I'll see what we can do. Now, would you mind just telling me a little about the job you're in at the moment?'

Jean: 'Well, most of the day I'm doing filing, a bit of Xeroxing, a bit of typing, and sometimes I get one hour a day on the switchboard when the other girl goes out to dinner.'

Interviewer: 'Tell me, I know it sounds a silly question, but what's so special about switchboard operating?'

Jean: 'I just like speaking to people on the phone. I use my brother's telephone sometimes, and I like that. I've always tried to speak well, you see. You have to for that job. I did think of elocution lessons, but I never got round to it.'

Interviewer: 'The trouble is Jean, the P.O. don't train telephonists any more, since they went on to S.T.D. and most other places want girls with experience.'

Jean: 'I did ring up all the hospitals as they need people, but they wouldn't take me when they heard I was only seventeen and didn't have any experience.'

Interviewer: 'Oh, that was a very good idea. I see you've really been trying. I do hate to disappoint you, but I think the best I can do is find you general office with relief switchwork.'

Jean: 'Filing again?'

Interviewer: 'I'm afraid, Jean, that I really haven't got anything else for you, but I could put you on the list of telephonists. How would that be?'

Jean: 'Well, I suppose so.'

Interviewer: 'But I'll tell you what, Jean, why don't we find you a job with a day release, and you could learn to be a secretary?'

Jean: 'Go to college? Oh no, I wouldn't want to.'

Interviewer: 'Of course it's entirely up to you. But if I was you, I'd always go for the jobs that have a day release, because it shows that they're good employers.'

Eventually she agreed on a job in a small civil engineers' office, but she left the room without much enthusiasm, thanking the officer who apoligised and wished her the best of luck.

from *A Working Life* by Polly Toynbee (adapted)

For Discussion

1 In what respects do Jean and Michael give good interviews?

2 What kinds of questions might the interviewer have asked to help them to give better interviews?

3 Jean is disappointed this time in her search for work as a telephonist. What advice would you give her to help her in the future?

4 What do you think Michael means when he says he wants to 'get on'?

5 Why do you think Jean is so interested in being a telephonist?

PUNCTUATION: Full Stops (to show abbreviations)

Notice how in several of the extracts in this Unit, the writers have used full stops to show that words have been abbreviated. Sometimes they have been abbreviated to single letters.

For example, in Polly Toynbee's article, one of the interviewers talks of the 'P.O.' and 'S.T.D.'. What are these short for?

Suggest other examples.

Colon (:)

1 In 'Students Talking' Paul Tufnell writes:

Most of us have fantasies: we have marvellous dreams for ourselves . . .

Here he is using a colon to *join two statements where the second statement expands on the first.* In other words, the second statement tells us what kinds of fantasies we have.

Another example would be:

I like Greece for many reasons: it's got perfect weather; it's got delightful people; and there's lots of interesting places to see.

Again, the second part of the sentence expands on the first part.
Notice two other similar uses of the colon:

2 *To introduce a quotation:*

According to Shakespeare: 'The quality of mercy is not strained . . .'

3 *To introduce a list:*

He bought a number of items: breakfast cereal, powdered milk, cheese, bacon and eggs.

Rewrite these sentences using colons, full stops, and semicolons if you think they are necessary. (Before you do this, chat again about the use of the semicolon.)

1 He joined the RAF she joined the WRNS.
2 They like all kinds of music pop music, classical music, light music and jazz.
3 HM The Queen declared the meeting open.

4 The writer expresses his own opinion very clearly 'This is a terrible thing for anyone to do.'
5 It's easy to see this place is dangerous there have been many crimes committed here since last Christmas.

A Interviewing Parents or Older Friends

Collect information about their attitudes towards work. These are some of the questions you might use in your interviews, but be sure to adapt your questions as you go along so as to get people chatting and relaxed:

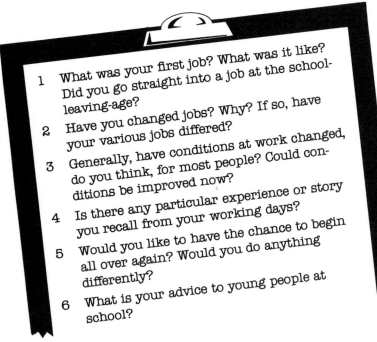

1 What was your first job? What was it like? Did you go straight into a job at the school-leaving-age?

2 Have you changed jobs? Why? If so, have your various jobs differed?

3 Generally, have conditions at work changed, do you think, for most people? Could conditions be improved now?

4 Is there any particular experience or story you recall from your working days?

5 Would you like to have the chance to begin all over again? Would you do anything differently?

6 What is your advice to young people at school?

Later, put your findings together as a group, and then write your own individual reports.

B Working Plans

Discuss your own hopes and ideas for work and careers. Talk about the reasons why they appeal to you, and also about the problems involved. Then make a list of any questions you may have regarding such work – including, for example, questions about training and qualifications, prospects, and conditions of work.

As you talk together, you should try to add to each other's lists of questions. These might be questions to which you can find answers in books and pamphlets, and also questions about which you would need to talk to other people.

Try to include plans and ideas which you do not necessarily think are very practical, as well as some ideas that you think are more realistic.

After you have discussed the ideas with each other prepare your own individual reports, in two parts:
    1 plans, and
    2 questions.

C Letter Writing

After you have compared your reports with the rest of the class, write a short letter of inquiry to any person or institution (such as a personnel officer or a college) requesting further details about either a course or a job in which you are interested. Discuss the letter with the rest of the class before you send it.

Later, compare the answers you have had to your letters, and also talk about the various other ways in which you can find the answers to your questions in item B, above.

15 In the News

The edited version of Waud's sketch of the wounded after the battle of Antietam, 1862, in the American Civil War

General Haig: 'the photographer is restricted to giving us one impression at one time'

Listening Comprehension

Photographs in the News

This is an extract from a talk given on television by a former editor of The Sunday Times.

It is sometimes thought that the arrival of the moving picture made the still image obsolete. I believe, quite to the contrary, that the still image has never been more powerful. Of course television's moving pictures have broken the monopoly of the newspaper photograph and drawing; but it has not killed them, because there is something of value in both mediums.

The picture on p. 149 shows a police chief in Saigon executing a Vietcong prisoner. It is an image you will be able to recall for a long time. Taken [in 1969], anyone who saw it then would still have been able to recall it. That shooting was shown on television too, but it is the still, the moment frozen in time, that has been absorbed in the mind: the most important gunshot of the war not because it was *heard* around the world but because it was *seen*.

The difference between the moving picture on television and the still image is that the moving picture cannot easily be recalled to mind or pondered on. The still picture has an affinity with the way we remember. It preserves for ever a finite fraction of the infinite time of the universe. It is easier to recall an event or a person by summoning up a single image – capturing a single point in time.

... Legions of reformers have followed the example of Jacob Riis, a New York newspaper reporter who despaired of making people believe that the New York sweat-shops and slums were as bad as he in words had said they were. In 1888 he taught himself to use a camera, bought some of the newly invented flash-powder and in a series of raw photographs proved his point. He won immediate reforms which improved the lives of thousands of people. Since Riis the documentary photograph has had many triumphs, such as the documentation of the American Mid-West dust bowl of the Thirties.

The descriptive photograph offers ... detailed observation as well as emotional appeal. It is ideal for newspapers. It can unpeel reality. A girl goes for a walk, but she is a thalidomide child held up by a harness.

The power of the still image is such that the history of picture journalism is replete with temptations to exploit it as well as to use it for enlightenment; and this was the case even before photographs became the main source of illustrations in newspapers. In fact, it was Britain which gave illustrated journalism to the world, for the 'Illustrated London News' was the first illustrated paper in the world and was first published, as a weekly, in 1842. The paper was full of engravings and was a sell-out from the start. It is still being published today, but as a monthly.

The American Civil War in the 1860s was photographed quite extensively but the camera's exposure time was too slow to catch action. The photographers were also handicapped because they needed a horsedrawn covered wagon to transport their precious chemicals and fragile developing equipment. By contrast, all the special artist needed was a horse, pencil and sketchbook – and courage. It was the special artists' drawings which made the news pages.

Alfred Waud, who sketched his way through the American Civil War with his British passport in his pocket, found that on several occasions the action came too close for comfort; for instance, at the battle of Fredericksburg. He also sometimes fell foul of censorship, not so much from local military commanders but from his editors back at base. One of his sketches showed the wounded being carried off after the battle of Antietam in 1862. It showed, on the left, surgeons treating a soldier after an amputation and, on the stretcher, another soldier who had clearly lost a leg. But when the engraved version of the drawing appeared in 'Harper's Weekly' two alterations had been made. The stretcher case appeared with his good, left leg nonchalantly crossed over his bandaged stump, and the patient on the left of the picture had been tactfully turned around. Waud was furious that the public was being sheltered from the brutal facts of war, especially in view of the dangers he himself faced in providing his sketches.

But the tendency to manage the news continued. In the Boer War, home-based artists drew so-called Boer 'atrocities' to distract attention from British defeats.

... The photographer is restricted to giving us one impression at one moment. That is why it is important to be sceptical about accepting the photographic image as a single verdict.

The power of the photographer to manipulate the images he presents us with is immense: he does not need an off-guard or unflattering moment to ridicule or condemn a subject. Photographing from below can accentuate the tense neck, the bullying chin, the arrogant head angle.

But it is not only the photographer who can make us see people in a particular way. A lot happens between the click of the shutter and the printing of the image. The photograph passes through many sieves. There is the picture editor, who selects perhaps six shots from 60, and probably a managing editor or editor, who makes a final choice.

I have tried to give you some necessary cautions about photojournalism, and there are others. But we must keep a sense of perspective. When I hear snooty remarks about photojournalists I think of one of their greatest achievements: the objective presentation of war and its consequences. Their pictures have told many truths: about the Second World War, about the Korean War and about the Vietnam War ... Contrast that with World War One, when newspapers did not show the realities of trench warfare. The whole Establishment, including the press, prevented people from seeing what was really going on and distracted them with a fanfare of patriotic bugle calls. We would regard it as unthinkable today *not* to show pictures as important as these – thanks to some more open attitudes, and also to the brave photographers who are prepared to be there, to risk everything in order to capture an image they believe will reveal a universal truth and hold it fast for ever.

Harold Evans

'An image you will be able to recall for a long time'
The Vietnam War: a police chief in Saigon executes a Vietcong prisoner, 1969

QUESTIONS

After listening to the passage a second time, write your answers to these questions.

1   What is the main point that the writer makes about the photograph of the Vietcong prisoner being shot?

2   A news reporter was one of the first people to use photographs as a way of making people believe the truth about bad social conditions. Explain briefly what he photographed.

3   What was the first journal to use illustrations? Roughly when was this?

4   The engraving of the battle of Antietam was 'edited' before being used in a newspaper. Say briefly how it was edited and why.

5   The writer gives two examples of wars in which illustrations were deliberately used to mislead the public about what was really going on. What were the two wars?

6   The writer says that a photograph can 'unpeel reality'. Explain what this means.

7   How does the writer think a photographer can influence and even mislead the public?

8   In what ways does the writer think that an editor can influence and mislead the public when publishing a photograph?

9   In which wars does the writer think that photojournalists have given great service to the public?

10 Explain in a sentence or two what you think is the main point made by Harold Evans.

THE BIG STORY

All newspapers give great prominence to certain stories. Here is an example – a set of four reports of one continuing story, covering a period of three days.

Story of a Mafia boss who became the victim of bloody ambition . . .

Killing of the Godfather

The 12-year reign of Mafia godfather Paulo "Big Paul" Castellano ended in a hail of bullets on Monday night.

Castellano, 70, was shot dead as he stepped from his Lincoln Continental limousine at Sparks Steak House on New York's 46th Street.

Three men in trench coats and fedora hats sauntered over, drew semi-automatics, and pumped six bullets into Castellano and his heir-apparent, Thomas Bilotti, at point-blank range.

It was a classic Mafia killing and ended a story that began in Sicily . . .

by NICHOLAS DAVIES
Foreign Editor
and JOHN McSHANE

Paulo Castellano was born into poverty a few years after his penniless parents arrived in New York.

Sixty years later he had reached the height of his ambition and became Cappo di Tutti Capi – the boss of all bosses of the Mafia.

He had achieved the American Dream – Sicilian-fashion.

Paulo lived in a two million dollar mansion, a copy of the White House in the most exclusive part of New York.

Television cameras guard every entrance and sophisticated burglar alarms protect the house and grounds.

The 70-foot living room is littered with antiques and priceless paintings. There is a large indoor swimming pool.

It was from this lavish mansion, staffed by six armed guards, that Big Paul ran the Mafia.

The key to his success was family.

Carlo Gambino, model for the film *The Godfather*, was his cousin and Paulo married Gambino's elder sister Caterina.

In 1929 Paulo became an apprentice butcher.

During the next ten years, backed by the might of the Mafia, he rose to be the biggest meat and poultry wholesaler in North America.

Butcher

During Prohibition days Paulo rode shotgun for his cousin on illicit alcohol deliveries.

He quickly learned to butcher the victims his cousin selected – and became the perfect Mafia man.

Paulo came to prominence as a potential Mafia leader in 1957 when he was among 100 gangsters caught in a New York police swoop on a crime convention.

Six years later Big Paul had risen to the rank of an under-boss in the Gambino family.

In 1976 he was snapped in a controversial picture with Frank Sinatra backstage at a theatre. Castellano and the singing star, who had always denied links with organised crime, were shown surrounded by underworld figures.

Shark

That year Gambino died of a heart attack . . . and time began to run out for "Big Paulo," robbed of his protector.

protection, pornography and drug trafficking.

Murder

Big Paulo and his cohorts also found the time to carry out 25 gangland killings.

But the law's net was closing.

Last February, Castellano and the heads of the other four New York Mafia families were charged with operating a "board of directors" for organised crime.

Castellano was also awaiting trial for murder.

But Mafia justice got to him first.

The mob killings are believed to signal a power takeover bid by young members of the Gambino family.

THE HEIR: Aspiring Mafia boss Thomas Bilotti, gunned down in a New York Street.

Within two years Castellano was indicted as mastermind of a loan shark syndicate.

In 1980 Castellano's son-in-law disappeared and "Big Paul" was suspected because the missing man had two-timed on Castellano's daughter.

Castellano was later indicted for murder but promptly released on three million dollar bail.

For the next four years Castellano went into retreat and masterminded his vast empire from his lavish mansion. He continued to run the meat trade as well as a big slice of New York's construction industry, road haulage, property and the city's garment trade.

According to police, he also continued the Gambino family's illegal activities – loan sharking,

from *The Mirror*, 18 December 1985

THURSDAY

Mafia bosses backed Castellano slaying

By Ian Ball in New York

Paul Castellano, Mafia "Boss of Bosses" and head of the Gambino "Family," was slain with the approval of heads of New York's four other "families," according to the State's top expert on organised crime.

Ronald Goldstock, director of the Organised Crime Task Force, said the kingpins of the Genovese, Luchese, Bonanno and Colombo rings apparently endorsed the efficient execution of Castellano and his bodyguard on a mid-Manhattan street on Monday night.

"Castellano was an important person and there was a possibility he could take all of them down. He was involved in one racketeering trial and facing other prosecutions that could have tied him up for three or four years.

"He couldn't provide leadership and the mob was losing money. Virtually everyone in the mob would say, "We're better off he's dead," said Mr Goldstock.

Early dinner

"Big Paul" Castellano, 73, was on trial for murder-conspiracy and car-theft when he was shot as he arrived for an early dinner in a favourite steak house in the heart of the fashionable East Side of Manhattan.

He faced almost certain conviction on at least one charge – tantamount to a life sentence for a man in his 70s. So would he co-operate to obtain leniency? Was he about to become useless as a leader?

Federal and state authorities said yesterday that they suspected New York Mafia leaders had come up with positive answers to both questions.

In addition, Castellano had shown signs of becoming a sloppy mob boss.

A man who had not seen the inside of a jail for 54 years was suddenly enmeshed in legal problems. He had allowed the FBI to outwit his personal security operations to plant listening

devices in his mansion in Staten Island.

The tapes are to be used as evidence in a forthcoming trial against the Mafia "Commission."

'Young Turks'

Meanwhile a fundamental problem remains to be resolved – the conflict between the old guard, which feels the organisation should turn more to white-collar crime such as labour racketeering, and the young Turks, who fear that others are taking over the high profit drug trafficking and loan sharking areas.

The leader of this renegade group has been identified as John Gotti, 45. He was missing yesterday from his comfortable but unpretentious home in the New York borough of Queens.

Next month, Gotti, his brother and seven others are due to go on trial on racketeering charges stemming from a series of murders, hijackings and armoured-car robberies dating to 1968.

from the *Daily Telegraph*, 19 December 1985

Epitaph for a mobster

U.S. Lawmen armed with cameras and notepads staked out the Mafia's "in house" funeral parlour in New York today.

They monitored hundreds of prominent underworld figures arriving to pay their last respects to Big Paul Castellano, the 70-year-old Mafia godfather gunned down by fellow gangsters on a crowded New York street.

Castellano's funeral, which promises to be a 20s-style spectacle, is scheduled for tomorrow.

Scores of gangland chiefs turned up at the Castellano mansion in Staten Island in chauffeur-driven Cadillacs and Lincolns.

At the Cusimano and Russo funeral home in Brooklyn, to which the Mafia forcibly "retires" its people from time to time, an endless stream of flowers arrived throughout the night. Some bouquets were so voluminous it took two, and often three, men to carry them.

CASTELLANO: last respects.

from The London Standard, 19 December 1985

FRIDAY

MOBS PAY THEIR RESPECTS TO THE GODFATHER

BY MIRROR REPORTER

Sinister figures in dark glasses, snap-brim hats and black overcoats with velvet collars paid homage yesterday to a fallen Mafia chieftain.

They came in their long, black limousines to the New York funeral home where 70-year-old "Big Paul" Castellano lay in state.

An endless flood of floral tributes followed them to the Cusimano and Russo funeral parlour in Brooklyn. Some were so large it took three men to carry them.

Watching from a discreet distance in their less-luxurious cars were FBI agents and detectives noting down the identities of the 800 mourners.

Relief

They were keeping a particular lookout for John Gotti, 45, a captain in Castellano's Gambino family, who is a suspect in the shooting of the "boss of bosses" and his chief aide earlier this week.

The FBI refused to say later whether Gotti was at the wake. "It was a routine surveillance, nothing more," one agent said.

Castellano was buried later at a private ceremony. And it brought a sigh of relief from his former underworld colleagues.

He was on trial for operating a car-theft racket and faced further charges.

He was rumoured to be preparing to do a deal to save himself from a long sentence he was unlikely to survive.

BIG PAUL: "Doing a deal"

from The Mirror, 20 December 1985

153

For individual work

A Presenting Information to the Reader

Reporters are trained to give precise and clear information to their readers. Most news stories can be expected to answer these questions:

- What has happened?
- When?
- Where?
- To whom?
- How?
- Why?

Write down the answers to these questions in each of the four different news stories, taking one story at a time.

B Style of News Reporting

Reporters are usually expected to write their stories in clear and simple language. Generally this means:

- using short words,
- writing short sentences,
- writing short paragraphs, and
- beginning with the main piece of information.

Which of the news stories do you think most succeeds in following these rules? Explain why.

Later, compare your answers with the rest of the class.

SPORTS STORIES

Sports reporting is a major part of all newspapers. Here are two examples. Working together in small groups or in pairs, read them and discuss them.

THE RUN MACHINE

from MIRROR REPORTER in Adelaide

UNIL GAVASKAR, the little Indian opener, became the most prolific batsman in Test history when he hit a record-breaking 31st century and topped 9,000 runs yesterday.

He went well clear of Sir Donald Bradman's 29 Test hundreds and is now way ahead of the game's greatest Test run scorers with his appetite for cricket still keen in his 37th year.

Gavaskar hit an unbeaten 166 in Adelaide yesterday as India also achieved a record 520 total against Australia in the drawn first Test.

But last night the little man played down his achievements, pointing out that, while Bradman took only 51 Tests to reach his 29 tons, he himself took 94 to equal that mark.

"Don Bradman was a superman," he said. "I don't think you can compare me with him."

But tributes still poured in. Clive Lloyd, retired captain of West Indies against whom Gavaskar scored 12 of his tons, said: "He has no apparent weakness. He is a run machine."

Kapil Dev, the current Indian captain – a role which exposed Gavaskar's one apparent weakness when he led the side – said: "Sunny has determination and a coolness of mind. That's how he's got to 9,000 runs."

Gavaskar reached his mark yesterday during a last-wicket stand of 94 with Shivlal Yadav which just added to the agonies of current Aussie cricket.

LETTING RIP: Gavaskar on his way to 166 – David Boon can only admire.

from *The Mirror*, 18 December 1985

Kite grounded

Southampton 1
Tottenham 3

By BRIAN SCOVELL

Marc Falco beats Phil Kite to score Tottenham's first goal

SOUTHAMPTON goalkeeper Phil Kite had a disastrous home debut at a rain-swept near-deserted Dell last night.

Kite's early mistakes cost his team two goals and enabled Spurs to qualify for the semifinal of the Screen Sport Super Cup where they meet either Everton or Norwich depending on the result of Spurs final group match against Liverpool.

Criticism

Last week Spurs lost 1-0 in their Milk Cup replay at Portsmouth and manager Peter Shreeve criticised them harshly last month after losing a League game 1-0 at the Dell. In 300 minutes of football on the south coast they hadn't scored a goal.

The hapless Kite, who once had a trial for Spurs, soon changed all that. He replaced Peter Shilton, who was suffering from a calf strain, and in the ninth minute he let a straightforward header from Clive Allen bounce back to Mark Falco who hammered it into the roof of the net. That was a third goal for the leading scorer in the competition.

Kite's positioning was at fault when a long pass from Ossie Ardiles put Allen away in the 20th minute. Allen, who had been allowed to run on by two defenders, looked up, saw Kite off his line and chipped over his head with a superb piece of skill.

Near the end, Kite made two fine saves with his legs to stop Richard Cooke, a 64th minute sub for Allen, but by then it was too late.

Spurs, desperately needing a good result to restore confidence, abandoned their offside tactics and used skipper Steve Perryman as a sweeper. The ploy was designed to counter the pace of Danny Wallace and he only escaped once to score in the 54th minute, tucking in Steve Moran's low cross.

Shreeve said: 'It's the first time I've used a sweeper and Steve was the best player on the pitch. He was immaculate. It was a valuable win for us and it helped morale.'

Dave Leworthy was unmarked when he headed in the third goal in the 83rd minute after coming on as a 75th minute replacement for Ardiles who picked up a booking for fouling Jimmy Case.

The gate of 4,680 was the lowest so far in the tournament.

from the *Daily Mail*, 18 December 1985

For Discussion

1   Make brief notes showing how the writers of these stories have answered the questions outlined on page 154 (under the heading, *Presenting Information to the Reader*).

2   Does either of the writers follow the rules outlined on page 152 for the style of news reporting? Briefly explain.

3   Which story do you think is better written? Explain why.

Later, compare your answers with the rest of the class.

PUNCTUATION: Speech Marks

In earlier units, there have been many examples of the use of speech marks in writing conversation or dialogue. The extracts in this Unit show two other uses.

1   Speech marks are used to show the titles of books, plays, poems, films, newspapers, and so on.

For example: **Harold Evans refers to the 'Illustrated London News'.**

Other examples would be:

   He read 'Gone with the Wind' and then went to see 'Gandhi'. He enjoyed both of them.

Note   that in some books, including this one, titles are not given in speech marks but are printed in italics.

Note   also that when people are given special names and nicknames, these too are sometimes written in speech marks.

For instance, in the Mafia stories in this Unit the reporters have written **'Big Paul'** and **'boss of bosses'**, to emphasise that these are unofficial but popular names that have been given.

2   Speech marks are also used to show that a word is used in an unusual or special sense.

For example: Harold Evans writes that false pictures were made by the British in the Boer War to show Boer **'atrocities'**. He uses the speech marks here to show that the pictures did not really show any atrocities at all, since the pictures were entirely fictional.

Other examples would be:

   Big Paul 'delighted' everyone with his charm and personality.
   (Meaning the opposite – he scared people for reasons other than his charm or personality!)

   If the Mafia dislike you, they shoot you. That's what they call 'justice'.
   (Meaning it is not what *we* would call justice.)

THREE PROJECTS

1 Interview and News Report

Interview a student who has, say, achieved something outstanding in sports or athletics, or in the performing arts, or who has travelled extensively. As a class, interview him or her, make your notes, and then write up a short news story based on the interview.

In making your notes, use you own improvised shorthand and abbreviations. Do not ask the interviewee to speak slowly.

2 Comparing News Reports

Collect three or four papers published on the same day and compare their accounts of one story.

Compare the information they give, the style of presentation and the bias, if any, in the stories.

3 Bias in Reporting

Here is a set of facts.

They are based on a survey taken by the government's Office of Population, and they compare what is happening now with what was happening two years ago.

This information is based on a report published in 1985. For the purposes of this exercise, you should imagine that it has just been published.

a) Write a news story based on this information, writing it in such a way as to make very clear to the reader that the news is bad and something should be done about it.

b) Then write a second version of the same story in such a way as to suggest that there is nothing very much to be alarmed about.

The information is based on surveys carried out with 10,000 children in 300 secondary schools.

	Now	Two years ago
Girls at 15 who smoke	24%	15%
Boys at 15 who smoke	28%	26%
Percentage of all school pupils who smoke	22%	19%
Percentage of		
a) boys	a) 31%	a) 26%
b) girls	b) 28%	b) 28%
who smoke regularly at 16		

Other information in the survey.

Child smokers generally have parents, brothers or sisters who smoke.

Many children think smoking is only harmful if you smoke a lot.

Children aged 11 to 15 are smoking approximately 25 million cigarettes a week.

16 *Candidates*

PARLONS paper company

require a

lively young person for general training in all branches of our expanding business. We buy and sell all kinds of paper. We need an applicant who is:

- prepared to travel
- willing to start on the ground floor
- pleasant and hard-working.

Excellent opportunities in the long term for the right person, but academic qualifications are less important than the right attitudes.

Starting salary approximately £5,500 per annum.

Apply by letter to the Personnel Manager, Parlons Paper Company Ltd., Industrial Way, Foxbourne, Foxshire.

A large number of candidates apply for the above job. Here are four of the applications, their references and the interviewer's reports on their first interview (with the Personnel Manager).

For Group Work

1 Read the letters of application that follow and discuss which ones impress you:
   a)   for the layout of the letters;
   b)   for the information given in the letters;
   c)   generally, as good candidates for the job.

Also make a note of any way in which you think the letters could be improved.

29 Barlows Crescent
Foxbourne
Foxshire
2E11 9TR

10th June 1988

The Personnel Manager
Parlons Paper Company
Industrial Way
Foxbourne
Foxshire

Dear Sir
         I was very interested in your advertisement for a young person for general training in your company. I am 16 years old and am leaving Foxbourne Secondary School as soon as I have finished my GCSE exams this month.

         I am taking exams in English, Maths, Metalwork, Movement, and Social Studies. My best subjects are Movement and Metalwork. I do not expect to get a high grade in any of the other subjects but I have done good work at school in other ways. For example, I have won the silver and gold awards of the Duke of Edinburgh Award Scheme for mountaineering. I have also played this year for the school's football team (the first eleven), and the second eleven for the school in cricket.

         My interests are body-building, games of all kinds, walking, mountaineering and travelling. I haven't yet travelled very far but I will do.

         If I am not able to get a job I will either do more studies at school in the sixth form or go to the local technical college. But I would prefer a job where I can start to see more of the world and start to learn how to do different things. That is why I hope you will give me an interview for your position.

         I thank you for your consideration of my application.

                  Yours faithfully
                  George Turner

                  George Turner

52 Cranstead Buildings,
Foxbourne,
Foxshire.
10th June 1988

The Personnel Manager
Parkons Paper Company,
Industrial Way,
Foxbourne

Dear Sir,
   I am 17 years of age and am just finishing a one-year course in business studies at Foxbourne Technical College. Last year I completed my secondary education at Foxbourne Secondary School, obtaining the following examination grades:

English, Grade B
Maths, Grade D
History, Grade C
French, Grade E
Domestic Science, Grade C
Social Studies, Grade E
Geography, Grade F

This year I have studied the following:

English for office and industry,
Maths
Office Practice
Accounts
Shorthand and Typing
Principles of Business Law

I am taking my exams in all these subjects this month and I think I will do quite well in them.
   I enjoy travelling, and have already travelled around most of Europe with my family on holidays. I get on well with almost everyone and have done a lot of things at school where I have been given responsibilities. At College I have been a member of the Students' Social Committee.
   I hope you will consider giving me an interview.
      Yours very faithfully, Lisa Rowlandson,
   Lisa Rowlandson (Miss)

Dear Sir,

Re your vacancy for a 'lively young person'

I would be most grateful if you would consider my application for the above post. I enclose my curriculum vitae and wish only to stress that I am lively, young, hopeful and keen to go places. I look forward to your reply.

Yours faithfully,

M. Croall

Martin Croall

Curriculum Vitae:

Martin Croall,
102 Lexham Gardens,
Foxbourne,
Foxshire.
Born: 14th July 1971.

Educated: Foxbourne Secondary School 1982 to 87.

Exams passed: 1987

English	Grade D
History	Grade E
Maths	Grade F
Social Studies	Grade E
Drama	Grade C
Movement Studies	Grade C

Educated: Foxbourne Technical College 1985 to 86.

Course of study: GCSE in English, Maths, Accounts, Commerce, History.

Other qualifications and interests:

English Speaking Board grade 2 exam, with distinction, passed 1987.

Member of college drama group.

Producer of Christmas entertainment at College for local old people.

Enjoy reading all kinds of novels and watching all kinds of films.

Produced a film at school in my fourth year with the school film club.

Referees:

1) M.J.Swainford, M.A. (Mrs)
Headmistress,
Foxbourne Secondary School,
Linton Avenue,
Foxbourne

2) J.L.Mcdonald, B.A. (Mr)
Head of General Studies Dept
Foxbourne Technical College,
Foxbourne

9 Leys Avenue
Foxbourne
Foxshire
IG12 9ET
10th June 1988

The Personnel Manager
Parlons Paper Company
Industrial Way
Foxbourne

Dear Sir or Madam

   I was very interested in your advertisement in the 'Foxbourne Herald' for a young person to train for a career with your Company. I hope you will consider my application.

I am 16 years of age and am just taking my GCSE exams in English, History, Social Studies, Geography, General Science and Dance. All my school reports have said that I am a good average student and so I hope to get quite good grades in all my subjects.

I have been a student at Foxbourne Secondary School since 1983 and I hope to get a job and leave school this summer. I may, though, go back to the sixth form at school after the summer.

I am very interested in starting a good career and I have been told that your company are very good employers.

            Yours faithfully,

                D. Panesar.

Daljit Panesar (miss)

Group work continued

2 *Now read the letters that follow, given by the school and college as* references *for the four candidates.*

   a) Are there any marked differences between what the school or college says, and what the candidates have said about themselves?
   b) Putting the letter of application with the reference, which candidates so far have made the best impression?

**Foxbourne
Education
Authority**

Foxbourne Secondary School

Linton Avenue

Foxbourne

19th June 1988

Our Ref KLK/JH
Your Ref PM/LTR/57

Dear Mrs McLafferty

Re George Turner

George Turner is now completing his fifth year at this School. He is taking his GCSE exams and he is expected to secure reasonable grades in English, Maths, and Social Studies, and to do outstandingly well in Movement Studies and Metalwork. He is not an academic student but he has real strengths in other ways and I have no hesitation in recommending him to your attention. He is adventurous and resourceful. For example, he has won awards from the Duke of Edinburgh Award Scheme for mountaineering and for leading a group on a journey across the moors. He is also an outstanding sportsman, and has played for the School at both soccer and cricket.

He is widely liked by both the students and the staff. It was not until his third year here that he began to develop his interests in sport and in outward bound activities, but these quickly led him to become an outstanding pupil in the School and a real leader. He is also very reliable. If he agrees to do something, then he does it properly and successfully.

He is modest and sensible, hard-working and keen. He has seldom been absent from School, and is always punctual, of good appearance and courteous in manner.

Yours sincerely

K.L. Knight M.A.
Deputy Headmaster

Mrs P McLafferty
Personnel Manager
Parlons Paper Company
Industrial Way
Foxbourne
Foxshire

**Foxbourne
Education
Authority**

Foxbourne Technical College

General Studies Department

Foxbourne

19th June 1988

Your Ref PM/LTR/57
Our Ref JLM/KY

Dear Mrs McLafferty

Lisa Rowlandson

Regarding your letter of the 16th requesting details of Lisa Rowlandson's work at this College, I am pleased to say that she has just completed a successful year's study in this Department. She is now taking our Diploma in Business Studies and we expect her to do well in all her subjects, including English, Maths, Office Practice and Accounts.

She came to us from Foxbourne Secondary School where her teachers reported well of her pleasant manner, good attitude to work, and quiet conscientiousness. She is not a really confident or outspoken student, but we believe that if she has the opportunities of finding her feet in a good job she will soon develop and prove herself.

All of the lecturers here speak well of her. She has worked hard in all her various subjects. She has also been a member of a small group of students who have organised dances and socials, and she has done this very well. She is quiet, efficient and fully reliable.

Yours sincerely

J.L. McDonald

J.L. McDonald B.A.
Head of Department

Mrs P. McLafferty
Personnel Manager
Parlons Paper Company
Industrial Way
Foxbourne Foxshire

**Foxbourne
Education
Authority**

Foxbourne Technical College

General Studies Department

Foxbourne

19th June 1988

Your Ref PM/LTR/57
Our Ref JLM/KY

Dear Mrs McLafferty

Martin Croall

Martin has just completed a good year at this College, studying for the GCSE in a
group of subjects in which he hopes to achieve higher grades than he achieved at
his school last summer. He has worked well and deserves to be successful.

He is a reasonably able student, but his real strength is his personality. He
speaks well, is confident and relaxed, enjoys people's company and has a lively,
go-ahead manner. It seems to many of his lecturers that he has the makings of
an excellent salesman or public relations officer.

He has also taken a very active role in a number of social events in his year with
us, including an entertainment for local old age pensioners. He did this very well,
in a style both friendly and efficient. He will be well worth your consideration for
any appointment.

Yours sincerely

J.L. McDonald

J.L. McDonald B.A.
Head of Department

Mrs P. McLafferty
Personnel Manager
Parlons Paper Company
Foxbourne
Foxshire

Foxbourne Education Authority

Foxbourne Secondary School

Linton Avenue

Foxbourne

19th June 1988

Our Ref KLK/JH
Your Ref PM/LTR/57

Dear Mrs McLafferty

Re Miss Daljit Panesar

Thank you for your enquiry regarding Daljit Panesar. She is a good pupil. She has worked well, done her best, and has had good reports from all her teachers. She is expected to do well in all her GCSE examinations this summer – English, General Science, History, Social Studies, Geography and Dance.

She has other strengths. She is a remarkably good organiser. For example, she has organised collections in the School for local charities. She has done excellent work helping to collect food and other gifts for a local orphanage at Christmas. She has also been a lively and reliable member of the School Dancing Group, travelling around with them and giving shows at various places in the community.

She is always punctual, and is very seldom absent. She always gives of her best, and is pleasant to work with.

Yours sincerely

K.L. Knight M.A.
Deputy Headmaster

Mrs P. McLafferty
Personnel Manager
Parlons Paper Company
Foxbourne
Foxshire

Group work continued

3 *Interviewer's reports*

All four of the applicants are selected for a first interview by the Personnel Manager.

Read the interviewer's reports that follow, and discuss:

a) Which candidates have given the best impression overall?

b) Which if any of the candidates have done either better or worse at the interview than their applications and references might have led you to expect?

c) If the Personnel Manager is expected to select two candidates to go forward for a final interview, which two candidates would you recommend her to select?

Later, compare your discussions with the rest of the class.

NAME	George TURNER

MANNER Quiet, quite relaxed, seemed to be both sensible and self-confident. Friendly. Spoke pleasantly and honestly. For example, he said that he had to spend hours on his letter of application and he took it back to his English teacher eight times for help and correction.

APPEARANCE Smart. Formally dressed. Clean.

QUESTIONS ASKED BY THE APPLICANT

Wanted to know a great deal about the Company and about the different things he would be expected to do in the first year. Seemed very pleased when I stressed that he would have to do a lot of practical work and no writing.

Said he was interested in a long-term future but not worried about it. When I asked him why, he said he preferred to take life as it comes!

Asked about salary, conditions of work and holiday entitlement. Wanted to know all about the Company's social facilities and was thrilled to hear about the sports and athletics club.

NEW INFORMATION GAINED ABOUT THE APPLICANT

Very interested in the national and international news. Spoke very confidently about the arms race. Obviously lively and interested in everything that goes on.

Also has had part-time (weekends) work at local supermarket stacking goods on shelves. Said he hates it but that he's learned something from it - to make sure he gets a good and interesting job.

GENERAL IMPRESSION

Pleasant, mature, resourceful.

NAME   Lisa ROWLANDSON

MANNER   Pleasant, sociable, talks well.

APPEARANCE   Smart, clean, sensibly dressed.

QUESTIONS ASKED BY THE APPLICANT

Wanted to know about hours of work, difficulties of getting from home to work, and wages and holidays.

Did not ask about any other facilities at work, such as social activities. Did not ask about prospects for the future but asked many good questions about her work for the first few years. Seemed very interested in all of it.

NEW INFORMATION GAINED ABOUT THE APPLICANT

Spoke very sensibly of both school and college, saying what she had enjoyed and what she had not enjoyed. All her comments were fair and to the point.

Spoke very well about hoping to travel when she is a little older. She obviously feels that she is still young and does not feel that she is ready yet for leaving home. But she looks forward to doing so later, she says. She said she would be very willing to do any extra studying in the evenings if we wanted her to.

GENERAL IMPRESSION

Steady, sensible, inexperienced, able.

NAME   Martin CROALL

MANNER   Mixture of nervousness and confidence. Could seem a little arrogant, perhaps because he is more shy than he thinks he is. Talks very well once he gets going and once he feels that he is liked and approved of.

APPEARANCE   Smart, clean.

QUESTIONS ASKED BY THE APPLICANT

Had a long list of excellent questions which he had obviously worked out and committed to memory. Wanted to know about the work he would start doing and also about the various prospects for the future. He asked how many of the 'people at the top' begin at the bottom, and also wanted to know what would happen to him if we decided not to promote him. I explained that there are no simple answers to these questions, but that we really do expect people to move up - that is how the Company works. He was pleased to hear this.

Asked if the Company had social facilities and was pleased to hear that we have.

NEW INFORMATION GAINED ABOUT THE APPLICANT

Has had a number of part-time jobs in local shops, and has enjoyed all of them. He now thinks he may have spent too much time on such jobs which could have been better spent studying for his exams. I asked what he thought he had gained from such jobs, apart from money and enjoyment, and he was not sure.

GENERAL IMPRESSION

Not quite as confident as he likes to think. Pleasant. Lively.

NAME   Daljit PANESAR

MANNER   Poised, speaks well, quietly self-confident.

APPEARANCE   Smart, clean.

QUESTIONS ASKED BY THE APPLICANT

Was most interested in the long-term prospects for the job. Said she did not mind what she did for the first few years, provided she was learning useful things and had a good chance of going places. Wanted to know how big the Company is, and how many young people start with us in any year. Said she was interested in travel and wanted to know where we would expect her to travel to.

I explained that she would not travel at all for the first few years and she accepted this.

Did not ask about the social facilities at work, but did ask very carefully about wages, holidays and conditions of work.

Asked if she would have a chance to meet any of the people she would work with if she was offered the job.

NEW INFORMATION GAINED ABOUT THE APPLICANT

She is writing letters to large numbers of local companies regarding the possibilities of work, and also to companies in other parts of the country. She is keen to know exactly what sort of qualifications we look for, and also whether she really ought to stay on at school or go to technical college to improve her qualifications.

She very sensibly used me as an opportunity for learning more about her prospects in general.

GENERAL IMPRESSION

Confident and sensible, thoughtful and intelligent.

FOR WRITING

1 Write your own letter of application for the same job or for any vacancy you have recently seen advertised.

2 Write the reference you would like your school or college to send on your behalf.

17 Turning Points

Bessie Smith c.1920 by Edward Elcha

The extracts in this Unit are all concerned with ways in which people's lives and careers suddenly change.

Three of the extracts are taken from biographies, and the fourth is from an autobiography.

Randolph Turpin

When Randolph Turpin was 23 he became the world middleweight boxing champion, beating the reigning champion Sugar Ray Robinson on points in a fifteen bout match in New York. That was in 1951.

Fifteen years later, he shot himself and died in Leamington in a small café owned by his wife, where he worked as a cook. He had been born in nearby Warwick, the youngest of five children, and his father died when he was a baby. His mother was poor, proud and hard-working...

Boyhood

When he was five years old, Randolph was sent to West Gate Council school where he quickly established himself as a leader. With only six teachers to look after 300 boys the school was, naturally, a tough training ground for the half-caste youngster.

But by the time he was twelve years old he could out-punch, out-run or out-climb any boy in the school. His prowess as an athlete and fighter soon had him tagged as 'Licker', a nickname he carried throughout his subsequent boxing career.

Turpin could possibly have developed into a top-class athlete. No other boy of his age could match him for speed, and he was so superior to his schoolmates that one year he was banned from taking part in the school's annual sports day. Physically, it seemed he could do anything, including leap-frogging over an unbroken line of nine or ten boys. His school friends would line up, bend their heads forward to waist level, and Turpin would then sail over the line with one gigantic leap. The West Gate teachers would often come out into the playground to watch him perform this almost daily ritual.

As a boy, Turpin was a superb, all-round sportsman and also developed into an outstanding swimmer. He could swim great distances under water, although he once nearly lost his life after being trapped by underwater reeds. He managed to wrench himself free, but was kept under so long that he permanently damaged an ear drum which left him partially deaf.

Turpin's closest friend at the time was Pete Price who had been the Wathen Street gang leader until Turpin chose to challenge him for the honour. The two boys decided to fight it out and Pete was actually getting the better of the exchanges until Turpin swung both fists round at the same time – and completely felled his friend.

The two were inseparable and were to remain life-long friends. Price later became a professional fighter – he fought under the name of Peter Parsons – and although he never showed exceptional promise, he often sparred with Turpin.

One of the earliest recollections Price has of Turpin dates back to when the two were about four or five years old. Pete can remember Randolph taking a very heavy fall in the road, and was amazed when he climbed to his feet, dusted himself down and then went on playing.

Turpin seldom shed tears. The few times he did come running into the house crying, mostly after he had been roughed up by bigger boys, his mother would push him away and shout, 'You get back out there and give it back to 'em. Let 'em see what the Turpins are made of.' This inborn toughness was later to stand Turpin in good stead when he was fighting for a living. And even towards the end of his career when he was unable to stop the punches landing on what was then a suspect jaw, he still refused to surrender, and fought back until he was exhausted.

Randolph Turpin in the World Title Fight, 1953

[*By the end of his life, Turpin had become heavily in debt to the Inland Revenue.*]

At the back of his mind Turpin still cherished the dream of that guest house in Wales. The mounting debts, however, offered little prospect of this dream ever coming true. Yet, desperate as he was for money at that time, he resisted the temptation to sell his treasured Lonsdale Belt, or the many magnificent trophies won during his amateur career.

It was only during the last months of his life that he made it known he would be prepared to consider offers. He expected to get up to £10,000 for them.

Nine months before his death he wrote to Jack Solomons asking him to sell the trophies for him. 'I am in cash trouble Mr J, but I am not begging,' he pleaded. A month later he wrote to the London promoter again, this time saying, 'I am at my wits end . . . ' He also asked Alex Griffiths to help to sell his world-title and Lonsdale Belts and suggested a price of £8,000. 'He told me he was going through a fairly rough period. I opened negotiations and promised to see him, but we never clinched the deal,' said Griffiths.

But then Turpin suddenly had a change of heart and decided he didn't want to sell the trophies. And in the subsequent farewell note to his wife, he wrote: 'They are yours. As long as you keep them, you have a part of me. Don't ever sell them.' Sadly, Gwen was forced to sell the Lonsdale Belt after his death, for a reputed £3,000 (in the summer of 1974 it was auctioned at Christies and was bought by a Birmingham businessman for £10,000).

On the surface the former world champion seemed resigned to his life as cook in the back-street café. He would greet regular customers cheerfully, and acknowledge the hesitant enquiries of newcomers, often overawed at being in the presence of such a famous personality. But he would refuse to be drawn into discussions about his career, excusing himself quickly to return to the kitchen to shift his pots and pans about. Those magnificent days of the early 1950s were a blurred memory . . .

Christmas 1965, however, was a happy time for him. As if to make up for lost time, he played with his daughters and threw his house open for brothers Dick and Jackie and their families.

But 1966 offered no fresh hope. Leamington Council were still pressing ahead with the plans to pull down the café. And the Inland Revenue were regularly demanding a settlement . . . On 14 May, another official-looking letter dropped through the letter box, and even before he opened it, Turpin sensed the contents. The final demand. It meant, pay up, or be taken to court.

from *The Tragedy of Randolph Turpin* by Jack Birtley

For Discussion

1. Apart from his income tax problems, what else probably destroyed Randolph Turpin?

2. In what ways did the toughness he had as a boy a) help him, and b) let him down in his later life?

3. Turpin had immense fame and renown when he was still young. Can you think of any other famous people whose good fortune later deserted them?

4. What is ironic about the fate of his Lonsdale Belt?

Bessie Smith

Bessie Smith became one of the greatest jazz singers of all times, 'Empress of the Blues'. This is how she started . . .

She was born in the railroad town of Chattanooga, Tennessee, in 1894, one of seven children of William Smith, a part-time Baptist preacher. The whole family lived in poverty, which remained an inescapable fact of black life even though nearly thirty years had gone by since the end of slavery . . . The eldest son of the family died before Bessie was born, and her father soon after. Her mother was dead by the time she was eight. Bessie and the other surviving children were brought up by the eldest sister, Viola. There was little money for food, and none for doctors; no interest in schooling; and not much chance of finding a job of any kind. Half of Chattanooga was black and facing the same problems, so there was no easy way out of the ghetto.

From the age of nine, Bessie sang on street corners for nickels. She had a naturally powerful voice, and her earnings made a useful contribution to the family needs. She sang everything, including Baptist hymns, with the same healthy exuberance. There was a good deal of enterprise in the Smith family; it was Clarence [her brother] who first succeeded in joining Moses Stokes's travelling show as a dancer and comedian. In 1912 he arranged for Bessie to have an audition. By then she would have been about eighteen, and, to judge by the photographs, touchingly eager and vulnerable, in spite of her years on the Chattanooga streets learning to look after herself. Apart from reading and writing she had learnt very little else.

The audition brought Bessie the first luck she had, because the cast included Gertrude Rainey and her husband, Will. Aside from the chance this gave Bessie to listen and learn from Ma Rainey, Mother of the Blues, this was the first time a jazz singer of high calibre had heard her sing. And when the Raineys broke away to join another troupe a few months later, Bessie went with them. Ma Rainey had no children of her own, and she treated Bessie like a daughter, which made it easy for Bessie to leave her family.

Ma Rainey was a short, stubby figure, who loved dressing up outrageously; she loaded herself with diamonds and gold. She took particular pleasure in a necklace of gold coins, of different sizes, from $2.50 to heavy $20 eagles, which she often kept on in bed for fear it would get stolen. Her face was kindly; and her smile, too, was benevolent, even though her large teeth were capped with gold, and there was something in her which frightened men . . .

'Boy, she was the horriblest-looking thing I ever seen,' Little Brother Montgomery reported.

She was a good person to work for none the less. She wasn't a soft touch for money if one of her troupe had lost his own while gambling, any more than Bessie was; but if someone was in trouble she helped out quickly enough. When someone asked her whether she had any money, she replied with a laugh that rumbled through her whole body, 'Honey chile, what you talkin' about? I got a roll big enough to choke on.' . . .

Ma didn't need to kidnap Bessie to get her out of Chattanooga, as some stories suggest. Bessie was already weary with wanting to get away. And she understood that it was only by leaving that she could help support her sisters, and the children they already had. It was a financial contribution she was to make . . . for the rest of her life.

To succeed in the entertainment business of the time, Bessie's most significant disadvantages were her size, the African cast of her features and the unfashionable blackness of her skin. The chorus line was expected to look as if tanned golden-brown and to have a slender build; and beauty was supposed to lie in small, European features. Bessie's early full-lipped loveliness was unacceptable. Irvin C. Miller (himself black) had her thrown out of the chorus line for not meeting these standards, which must have bruised her awakening confidence, but did not check her determination . . . People have to love themselves if they are going to survive, and Bessie was a survivor. If she was black, then black was good.

from *Bessie Smith* by Elaine Feinstein

For Discussion

1   What similarity was there between Bessie Smith's background and Randolph Turpin's?

2   What similarity does there seem to have been in their characters?

3   What was ironic about the way in which she lost her job with Irvin C. Miller?

4   In order to make a living in show business, what else did Bessie Smith have to be able to do, apart from sing?

Broadway, St Louis, *c.*1890

Jean Rhys

Jean Rhys in her thirties

Jean Rhys was born in Dominica in 1890 and came to England as a teenager. Her first ambition was to be an actress but it was as a novelist that she eventually achieved success. Her most popular novel was Wide Sargasso Sea, *a prequel to Charlotte Brontë's* Jane Eyre.

In this extract from a biography of Jean Rhys, she decides to study to become an actress.

She wrote to her father and told him she wanted to go to the Academy of Dramatic Art.

Her father said she could go, and she was happier than she had ever been in her life. For a time she stayed on at school, taking extra elocution and singing lessons from a young clergyman. He asked her why she wanted to go on the stage.

'I love the sound of words.'

'And?'

'I like it when the audience claps, and I adore everything to do with the stage.'

At the end of 1908 she . . . went to take her entrance examination for the Academy. People said she wouldn't pass, and though she insisted that she would she was very nervous. She recited 'The Bells'; the judges seemed very bored. But her luck held and she passed . . . Aunt Clarice put her into another Bloomsbury boarding house and left her to it.

She entered the Academy of Dramatic Art with thirty-four other students in January 1909. Again she had set out with high hopes; again what she remembered was discomfiture and disappointment. It was like school, but worse. This time she arrived in a skirt which was too long, so that she had to wear it tucked up at the waist. Aunt Clarice said she was so thin that no one would notice, but of course they all noticed straight away. Again most of the teachers ignored or disapproved of her. Her friends were foreigners like herself – an Australian girl, a half-Turkish girl – and they didn't last long. The only girl who was nice to her left, after a terrible row over the proper pronunciation of a word.

> 'Froth,' said the elocution master. 'Frawth,' said the pupil. For a long time they shouted at each other: 'Froth' – 'Frawth' – 'Froth' – 'Frawth'. I listened to this appalled . . . At last Honour said: 'I refuse to pronounce the word "froth". "Froth" is Cockney and I'm not here to learn Cockney.'

Honour was taken away and the elocution master left or was dismissed. 'I learnt nothing at the school of acting except the exact meaning of the word snob,' Jean wrote when she was old . . . She left the Academy as she had left school, 'without a qualm'.

from *Jean Rhys* by Carole Angier

And here is the same episode in her life as she herself wrote about it in her autobiography.

I had written to my father about my great wish to be an actress. and true to his promise he wrote back, 'That is what you must do'.

The Academy of Dramatic Art . . . hadn't been going very long when I went there. It had not yet become 'Royal'. I was surprised when I found I had passed the so-called entrance examination. My aunt, who disapproved of the whole affair, left me in a boarding-house in Upper Bedford Place, very excited and anxious to do my best. I was seventeen.

The Academy was divided into the A's, the B's and the C's. The A's were the new students, the B's were half way, and I never met any of the C's. Well-known actors and actresses would arrive to advise the C's, but we never saw them except in passing. When matinee idols like Henry Ainley arrived, the girls would haunt the passages hoping to catch a glimpse of them, but they would pass along quickly, and also one wasn't supposed to look.

The A's were taught by an actress whose Christian name was Gertrude. I have forgotten her surname. The B's we sometimes met in a room downstairs presided over by a woman called Hetty. Here you could get coffee and sandwiches and here I met several of the B's and came to dislike them. I thought them conceited and unkind. Once, when I left my furs behind and came back to fetch them, I heard someone say, 'Is this goat or monkey?'

I must confess that my furs, like all my clothes, were hideous, for my aunt's one idea had been to fit me out as cheaply as possible. When we bought my one dress, my everyday wear, the skirt was far too long, even for those days but she said to have it altered would be too expensive. I could tuck it up at the waist and because I was so thin nobody would notice. So apparelled, I set off to be inspected by the A's, the B's and the C's.

Miss Gertrude was quite a good teacher, I think. One of our first lessons was to learn how to laugh. This was comparatively easy. You sang the doh re me fah soh lah ti doh, and done quickly enough it did turn out to be a laugh, though rather artificial. Our next lesson was to learn how to cry. 'And now, watch me,' said Miss Gertrude. She turned away for a few seconds, and when she turned back tears were coursing down her face which itself remained unmoved. 'Now try,' she said. The students stood in a row trying to cry. 'Think of something sad,' whispered the girl next to me. I looked along the line and they were all making such hideous faces in their attempts to cry that I began to laugh. Miss Gertrude never approved of me.

We had lessons in fencing, dancing, gesture . . . and elocution. In the elocution master's class there was once a scene which puzzled me and made me feel sad. It upset me because the master, whose name was Mr Heath, was the only one except for the gesture woman who gave me the slightest encouragement or took any notice of me, and Honour, the pupil who quarrelled with him, was the only one I really liked. We had even been to a matinée together, accompanied by a sour-faced maid. We were reciting a poem in which the word 'froth' occurred, and Honour refused to pronounce the word as Mr Heath did. 'Froth' said the elocution master. 'Frawth' said the pupil. For a long time they shouted at each other: 'Froth' – 'Frawth' – 'Froth' – 'Frawth'. I listened to this appalled. 'Froth' – 'Frawth' – 'Froth' – 'Frawth'. At last Honour said: 'I refuse to pronounce the word "froth". "Froth" is cockney and I'm not here to learn cockney.' Her face was quite white with the freckles showing. 'I think you mean to be rude,' Mr Heath said. 'Will you leave the class, please.' Honour stalked out, white as a sheet. 'We will now go on with the lesson,' said Mr Heath, red as a beet. There was no end to the scandal. Honour was taken away from the school by her mother, who had written a book on the proper pronunciation of English. Mr Heath was either dismissed or left. This gave me my first insight into the snobbishness and unkindness that went on.

Part of our training was that every week some of us would have to act a well-known scene before Miss Gertrude, and she would criticise it and say who was right and who was wrong. We usually played a scene from *Lady Windermere's Fan* or *Paula and Francesca* by Stephen Philips . . .

At that time there was a dancer called Maud Allen playing at the Palace Theatre. She was a barefoot dancer as they called it then, and wore vaguely classic Greek clothes. She was, of course, imitating Isadora Duncan. A lot of people in London were shocked by her and when in one of her dances she brought in the head of John the Baptist on a dish, there was quite a row and she had to cut that bit out. One day our dancing teacher said: 'Maud Allen is *not* a dancer. She doesn't even begin to be a dancer. But if I told her to run across the stage and pretend to pick a flower she would do it, and do it well. I'm afraid I cannot say the same of all the young ladies in this class, and I advise you all to go to the Palace and watch Maud Allen. It might do you a lot of good.'

During vacation from the Academy I went to Harrogate to visit an uncle. It was there that I heard of my father's death. My mother wrote that she could not afford to keep me at the Academy and that I must return to Dominica. I was determined not to do that, and in any case I was sure that they didn't want me back. My aunt and I met in London to buy hot-climate clothes, and when she was doing her own shopping I went to a theatrical agent in the Strand, called Blackmore, and got a job in the chorus of a musical comedy called *Our Miss Gibbs*.

from *Smile Please*, an unfinished autobiography by Jean Rhys

For Discussion

1   In what way was the dispute between Honour and Mr Heath an example of 'snobbishness'?

2   What did the dancing teacher think the students would learn from watching Maud Allen's performance?

3   Give two different examples from these two extracts to show that the teachers do not seem to have been much impressed by the students.

4   Give two different examples to show that the students do not seem to have much liked each other.

Now compare your answers with the rest of the class.

QUESTIONS *on all four extracts*

For individual work

1 Give two different examples to show Randolph Turpin's athletic abilities as a child, apart from his abilities as a boxer.

2 What shows that Turpin was deeply confused during the time leading up to his suicide?

3 Apart from her poverty, what was the main difficulty Bessie Smith had to overcome before she could be a success? Explain your answer.

4 Explain the meaning of:
a) vulnerable (paragraph 2 of *Bessie Smith*);
b) high calibre (paragraph 3 of *Bessie Smith*).

5 Give two different examples of the students' snobbery at the Academy of Dramatic Art when Jean Rhys was there.

6 Write out two sentences from different parts of the extracts that show that Jean Rhys did not often think people liked her.

7 Which of the three (Randolph Turpin, Bessie Smith, Jean Rhys) seems to have taken longest to discover their main talent?

8 Which of the three seems most to have enjoyed his or her childhood? Explain why.

9 Which of the three seems to have had the least hardships as a child?

10 On the basis of these extracts, which of the three do you find the most interesting person? Explain why.

_____ *BIOGRAPHICAL WRITING* _____

Make a short list of people whose biographies you would be interested to read. Use your local libraries to see how many books you can find about them.

Choose two or three people to read about, and before you start reading, make a list of a dozen or so questions to which you hope to find answers.

Later, organise your findings into an essay in which you compare one or two aspects of the persons' lives – you might for example write a comparison of their childhoods.

Or do a similar exercise with two or three people you know or could meet to interview.

18 The Influence of Film and TV

This Unit looks at the effects of film, video and TV upon young people and children.

Working in small groups, read the materials. Talk about each one before you move on to the next. Take time to discuss anything you find difficult in any of the materials, and also anything that you agree with and anything that you disagree with.

After your discussions, move on to the questions at the end of the Unit.

Boy dies trying to copy TV cowboy gallows scene

A 15-year-old boy died trying to copy the gallows scene he had seen on television, police said yesterday. In the Western, "The Hanged Man," a cowboy survives a hanging for a crime he did not commit.

But Glenn Miller died when he played out the part in his bedroom shortly after watching the scene on Tuesday night.

His brother, Brent, 12, found him hanging from his bunk bed with a leather thong round his neck tied to a dressing-gown cord.

Brent, who shared the room with Glenn, ran for help. His sister, Heather, tried to give the kiss of life.

Loved Westerns

Glenn's mother Mrs Anne Miller, 36, a divorcee, said at her home in York Road, Shepway, Maidstone, Kent, yesterday: "It all seems to have happened because of this film. I wish it had never been made." It was shown on ITV and began at 11.30 p.m.

"Glenn watched an awful lot of television. He was really keen on Westerns. I am heartbroken.

"I had been to the local club for divorced and separated people and popped back at about 11.30. Then I went for an Indian meal and arrived home to find the police and ambulance outside.

"Glenn had always been a bit of a handful for me. He set fire to the lounge once with his chemistry set and cut through an electric cable with a knife when he was only three ... Although he was the cleverest of my three children, he would do stupid things.

"Brent can remember nothing about the incident. He is too upset. He is now staying with his father because he cannot face going back into that room."

Tragic Influence

A police spokesman said: "This seems to be a tragic case of a youngster being influenced by a film. Apparently he had been watching the trailers for the film during the evening and then the start of the movie itself.

"In the film a cowboy is hanged, but survives and obviously this lad foolishly decided to try it for himself."

from the *Daily Telegraph*, 17 July 1978

184

Viewers do not copy Alf Garnett

The racial prejudices of Alf Garnett, the central character in the BBC TV comedy series *Till Death Us Do Part*, have little if any effect on the attitudes of viewers. This is the finding of the first *Annual Review of BBC Audience Research*, published today.

Till Death Us Do Part was intended to strike at racial prejudice by putting racist attitudes in the mouth of a selfish and vicious character. But it was soon feared that some viewers liked Alf Garnett, saw him as a folk-hero, and agreed with what he said.

The researchers have studied the comments of over 600 viewers, and it seems that most people think Alf Garnett is a bit of a fool and quite harmless.

The researchers say there is no evidence that the programme has had any effect at all. It does not seem to have made people more or less prejudiced.

According to the Review, most people in this country watch TV for 17 hours a week. Children aged 12 to 14 are the greatest viewers: they watch more than 24 hours a week. The 15 to 19 age group watch an average of 14 hours a week.

from *The Times*, 17 March 1975 (adapted)

'Children can't unwind from violence on TV'

DAILY TELEGRAPH REPORTER

Violence is common among young people because mentally and physically they cannot unwind from the excitement of violent films and television shows, according to Prof. Ivor Mills, a Cambridge endocrinologist or glands specialist. "Almost anything that is interesting to us produces an increase in adrenaline, famous as the 'fight or flight' hormone." he said. "With an increase in adrenaline, we become more interested in 'fight'."

"Some types of films hold our interest and get us excited, and when they are over, our excitement disappears. But with some young people, if their imagination is stimulated by violence, real fear and excitement are put into them and when the film is over, the excitement persists."

from the *Daily Telegraph*, 24 July 1977

BBC looks again at violence code
By SEAN DAY-LEWIS, TV and Radio Correspondent

THE BBC is looking again at its standards on the portrayal of violence, and the use of bad language particularly in television drama, Mr Alasdair Milne, managing director of BBC television, announced yesterday. Producers may be given new guidelines.

"There is no question of us losing our nerve, but there are things done daily in the theatre or on the cinema screen, not to mention written about in books, which television cannot attempt," he said.

Miss Monica Sims, head of children's programmes, is to be chairman of a group of programme makers who will evaluate the existing BBC guidelines on the portrayal of violence and recommend any necessary revisions. The report of the committee will be published.

Mr Milne said that it was more difficult to provide written guidelines on language, but the Annan Committee had recorded that it received more correspondnce on this than any other subject.

There had recently been a meeting between the governors and the drama heads at which the former expressed concern and it was evidence that "what was acceptable three or four years ago is not acceptable now" that Mr Ian Trethowan, the Director-General, had this week cancelled the scheduled BBC1 repeat of Barrie Keefe's play "Gotcha."

from the *Daily Telegraph*, 17 August 1978

Home Videos Censored

The Video Recordings Act comes into operation this month. It requires that all films released on video should be resubmitted to the British Board of Film Classifications. Its effect will be to kill films that the Board disapproves of. If the Board does not approve, then the video will not go on sale or on hire in the shops.

from *Liberties*, September 1985 (adapted)

What do you think?

A group of students did a survey on people's attitudes to the influence of TV, film and video. They spoke to 50 people, and this is what they found out.

Notes on graph

The vertical shows the number of people who answered YES to a question.

The horizontal shows the number of each question:

Question 1
Do you believe you have ever been harmed by watching any film? (No one answered YES.)

Question 2
Do you know any one who has ever been harmed by watching a film?

Question 3
Do you believe that some people may be harmed by watching films?

Question 4
Do you believe that most people may be harmed by watching films?

Question 5
Do you think there is too much violence on TV, film and video?

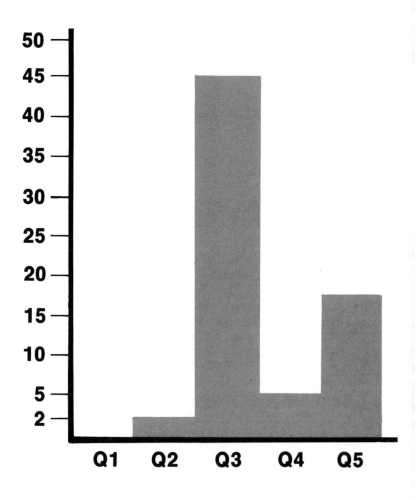

Minister claims under-sixes 'imitate violence seen on television'

A link between television violence and violent behaviour by children under six has been proved, a government minister claimed in the Commons yesterday.

Speaking in a debate on violent crime among young people, Mr David Mellor, the junior Home Office minister, agreed that there was no general connection between the increase in violence and the increase in TV viewing. But research had shown a link.

With the under-sixes it had shown that "violent films can give way to violent imitative behaviour." This was distressing because the formative years had an influence on later behaviour.

Secondly, a link had been established with backward children. Such children were more likely to seek pleasure in TV violence and were more influenced by it.

Mr Mellor said that even if research could not establish

firm links, "common sense leads us to suspect a constant diet of violence can encourage young people to engage in violence themselves."

In a speech last weekend, Mrs Thatcher suggested that television violence could be harming viewers, especially young people.

Mr Mellor said the Government's duty was not to dictate to the media but to voice public concern.

from *The Guardian*, 7 December 1985 (adapted)

TV FANTASY GIRL ORGANISED BINGO HOLD-UP

A GIRL school-leaver, longing for excitement to match the fantasy world of television which dominated her life, went out and organised an armed robbery, a court heard yesterday.

She recruited one man who had a shotgun, and another to act as getaway driver. The trio held up a bingo hall at Chelmsley Wood, Birmingham.

They stole £102, with the girl acting as look-out.

Yesterday, when all three pleaded guilty at Warwickshire Crown Court to theft and carrying a gun, Mr NIGEL CADBURY, defending the 16-year-old, said she was unbelievably immature and naive.

"She lived in her own fantasy world, completely detached from reality, and longed for glamour, excitement and adventure.

"She spent a great deal of her time watching television and was completely wrapped up in the programmes."

Sentence in June

Judge LEO CLARKE QC adjourned sentence on the girl until June for psychiatric and social reports. He ruled that she should not be named.

She was bailed on condition that she attends a social services activity programme.

JAMES PHIPPS, 21, of Chaffinch Drive, Chelmsley Wood, who provided the gun, got four years.

STEVEN SAVAGE, 21, of Landrail Walk, Chelmsley Wood, the getaway driver, got two years, 14 months of it suspended.

Mr COLIN MACKINTOSH for Phipps, said: "The girl talked him into carrying out the raid."

'Direct TV link'

Last night Mr John Beyer, organising secretary of Mrs Mary Whitehouse's National Viewers' and Listeners' Association, said the case illustrated the need for curbs on television violence.

"It is a tragedy. Television can influence the way young people, and immature people, can behave. This case is another example of a direct link."

He hoped the case would be noted by broadcasting authorities when they reviewed their codes, and might make them "admit for once that their programmes did have an effect.

"This young girl's life from now on will be affected. Her fantasy world has been created by television, and we will have to decide how many more of our young children are in this fantasy world."

from the *Daily Telegraph*, 7 December 1985

Government 'will not dictate' on TV violence

By OUR PARLIAMENTARY STAFF

MR MELLOR, Under-Secretary, Home Office, told the Commons yesterday that the Government did not intend to dictate to the television companies over the content of programmes but did have a duty to voice its concerns and those of the general public about what was shown.

Maintenance of standards was a matter for the broadcasting authorities.

They acted under a very clear statutory duty, he said, replying to a debate on violent crime by young people.

He urged the public to make their views known directly to the media when concerned about issues such as violence.

"At a time when more people are becoming alerted to worries about the influence on young children of a constant diet of violence on the screens, only a very small proportion actually take the trouble to make a complaint."

In the 12 months to last March only 1.3 per cent of complaints to the Independent Broadcasting Authority were concerned with violence. Mr Mellor said he understood similar figures related to the BBC.

Imitative behaviour

Mr Mellor said it was not easy to determine the impact of violence on television. But "commonsense must lead us to suspect that a constant diet of violence, particularly on young minds . . . , can encourage young people to go out and engage in violence themselves."

Research had confirmed that in children under six violent films could give rise to violent imitative behaviour.

from *The Times,*
7 December 1985